Psychiatry, Psychology, and Homosexuality

ISSUES IN LESBIAN AND GAY LIFE

Psychiatry, Psychology, and Homosexuality

ELLEN HERMAN

MARTIN DUBERMAN,
General Editor

CHELSEA HOUSE PUBLISHERS

New York ◼ Philadelphia

CHELSEA HOUSE PUBLISHERS

EDITORIAL DIRECTOR   Richard Rennert
EXECUTIVE MANAGING EDITOR   Karyn Gullen Browne
COPY CHIEF   Robin James
PICTURE EDITOR   Adrian G. Allen
CREATIVE DIRECTOR   Robert Mitchell
ART DIRECTOR   Joan Ferrigno
PRODUCTION MANAGER   Sallye Scott

ISSUES IN LESBIAN AND GAY LIFE
SENIOR EDITOR   Sean Dolan
SERIES DESIGN   Basia Niemczyc

Staff for PSYCHIATRY, PSYCHOLOGY, AND HOMOSEXUALITY
ASSISTANT EDITOR   Annie McDonnell
PICTURE RESEARCHER   Sandy Jones

Introduction © 1994 by Martin B. Duberman.

Library of Congress Cataloging-in-Publication Data
Herman, Ellen.
Psychiatry, psychology, and homosexuality/Ellen Herman; Martin Duberman, general editor.
    p. cm.—(Issues in lesbian and gay life)
Includes bibliographical references and index.
Summary: Describes the relationship between gay people and psychological experts and the struggle to define homosexuality.
ISBN 0-7910-2628-0
        0-7910-2977-8 (pbk.)
1. Gays—Psychology—Juvenile literature. 2. Homosexuality—Psychological aspects—Juvenile literature. [1. Gays—Psychology. 2. Homosexuality.] I. Duberman, Martin B. II. Title. III. Series.
HQ76.25.H46 1995
305.9'0664—dc20
94-44952
CIP
AC

FRONTISPIECE: Before activists successfully challenged the mental health establishment's diagnosis of homosexuality as "sick" or "abnormal," many lesbians and gay men found it easier to stay in the closet than to publicly proclaim their sexual orientation.

▦ *Contents* ▦

▦ *Issues in Lesbian and Gay Life* ▦

Other titles in preparation

How Different?

Martin Duberman

Just how different *are* gay people from heterosexuals? Different enough to support the common notion that they form a subculture—a shared set of group attitudes, behaviors and institutions that set them distinctively apart from mainstream culture? Of course the notion of the "mainstream" is itself difficult to define, given the many variations in religion, region, class, race, age and gender that in fact make up what we call "the heartland." And the problems of definition are further confounded when we broaden the discussion—as we should—from the context of the United States to a global one.

The question of the extent of "differentness"—of "queerness"—is subject to much debate, within as well as without the lesbian and gay world, and there are no easy answers for it. On one level, of course, all human beings share commonalities that revolve around basic needs for nurturance, affiliation, support and love, and those commonalities are so profound that they dwarf the cultural differences that set people apart.

Besides, it often isn't clear precisely what differences are under scrutiny. If we confine the discussion to erotic and affectional preference, then gay people are obviously different because of their primary attraction to members of their own gender. But what more, if anything, follows from that? Gay conservatives tend to believe that nothing follows, that aside from the matter of erotic orientation, gay people are "just folks"—just like everyone else.

But gay radicals tend to dispute that. They insist gay people have had a special history and that it has induced a special way of looking at the world. The radicals further insist that those middle-class gay white men who *deny* that their experience has been unusual enough to differentiate them from the mainstream are suffering from "false consciousness"—that they *are* more different—out of bed, as well as in—than they themselves would like to admit.

If one asked the average person what it is that sets gay men and lesbians apart, the likely answer would be that gay men are "effeminate" and lesbians "butch." Which is another way of saying that they are not "real" men or "real" women—that is, that they do not conform to prescribed cultural norms in regard to gender. It is true, historically, that "fairies" and "dykes" *have* been the most visible kind of gay person (perhaps because they were unable to "pass"), and over time they became equated in the popular mind with *all* gay people.

Yet even today, when gay men are often macho-looking body-builders and "lipstick" lesbians playfully flaunt their stereotypically feminine wiles, it can still be argued that gay people—whatever behavioral style they may currently adopt—are, irreducibly, gender nonconformists. Beneath many a muscled gay body still lies an atypically gentle, sensitive man; beneath the makeup and the skirts often lies an unusually strong, assertive woman.

This challenge to conventional gender norms—a self-conscious repudiation on the part of lesbian/gay radicals—is not a minor thing. And the challenge is compounded by the different kinds of relationships and families gay people form. A typical gay male or lesbian couple does *not* divide up chores, attitudes, or desire according to standard bi-polar "husband" and "wife" roles. Gay couples are usually two-career households in which an egalitarian sharing of rights and responsibilities remains the ideal, and often even the practice. And more and more gay people (particularly lesbians) are making the decision to have and raise children—children who are not trained to look to daddy for discipline and mommy for emotional support.

All this said, it remains difficult to *specify* the off-center cultural attitudes and variant institutional arrangements of lesbian and gay life. For one thing, the gay world is an extremely diverse one. It is not at all clear how much a black lesbian living in a small southern town has in common with a wealthy gay male advertising executive in New York City—or a transgendered person with either.

Perhaps an analogy is useful here. Literary critics commonly and confidently refer to "the Jewish novel" as a distinctive genre of writing. Yet when challenged to state *precisely* what special properties set such a novel apart from, say, a book by John Updike, the critics usually fall back on vague, catchall distinctions—like characterizing a "Jewish" novel as one imbued with "a kind of serious, kvetschy, doom-ridden humor."

Just so with any effort to compile an exact, comprehensive listing of the ways in which gay and lesbian subcultures (and we must always keep in mind that they are multiple, and sometimes at odds) differ from mainstream patterns. One wag summed up the endless debate this way: "No, there is no such thing as a gay subculture. And yes, it has had an enormous influence on mainstream life." Sometimes, in other words, one can *sense* the presence of the unfamiliar or offbeat without being able fully to articulate its properties.

Even if we could reach agreement on whether gay male and lesbian culture(s) stand marginally or profoundly apart from the mainstream, we would then have to account for those differences. Do they result from strategies adapted over time to cope with oppression and ghettoization? Or are they centrally derived from some intrinsic, biological subset—a "gay gene," for example, which initially creates an unconventional kind of person who then, banding together with like-minded others, create a novel set of institutional arrangements?

This interlocking series of books, *Issues in Lesbian and Gay Life,* is designed to explore the actual extent of "differentness" from mainstream values and institutions. It presents detailed discussions on a wide range of gay and lesbian experience and expression—from marriage and parenting, to history and politics, to spirituality and theology. The aim is to provide the reader with enough detailed, accurate information so that he or she can come to their own conclusions as to whether or not lesbian and gay subculture(s) represent, taken in their entirety, a significant departure from mainstream norms.

Whatever one concludes, one should always remember that differentness is not a disability nor a deficiency. It is another way, not a lesser way. Indeed, alternate styles of seeing (and being) can breathe vital new life into traditional forms that may have rigidified over time. Variant perspectives and insights can serve all at once to highlight the narrowness of conventional mores—*and* present options for broadening and revivifying their boundaries.

❖   ❖   ❖

In the 20th century, the profession of psychiatry became the chief arbiter of what is "normal" or "healthy" sexual behavior. Though claiming to be an "objective science," psychiatry has in fact shifted its definition of normalcy continuously through time—and usually in response to changing public mores rather than new data.

Ellen Herman's book is a comprehensive, subtle account of those shifts in psychiatric opinion—and the consequent effects on the self-esteem of gay people. Until roughly the last 20 years, the dominant view was that homosexual behavior was pathological and loveless. Most gay people internalized that definition, and the result was an enormous amount of pain and self-loathing; they blamed themselves rather than social oppression for their "perversion."

Herman tracks this history with a scholar's careful regard to evidence and in a lucid prose style that brings needed clarity to a complicated tale. Starting with the view early in the century that homosexuality was a disturbed "inversion," she traces the evolution of attitudes that culminated in 1973 in the American Psychiatric Association removing homosexuality from the category of "disease."

The fifty-year period in between saw a range of definitions—"arrested sexual development," "abnormal deviation," "'true' as opposed to 'situational' homosexuality," etc.; *and* of purported "cures," many of which bordered on the barbaric—aversion therapy, genital and brain surgery, hormonal and drug treatments. Herman shrewdly places these shifting views and treatments within the context of prevailing attitudes about what was considered "appropriate" gender behavior.

She does still more. She analyzes the work of those sexologists—from Freud to Kinsey to Irving Bieber to Evelyn Hooker—whose ideas proved so influential in establishing, or dismantling, prevailing categories of judgment. She shows how it gradually became understood that stigmatization itself—rather than any quality intrinsic to same-gender love—was responsible for the self-hatred and secrecy that made gay men and lesbians disproportionately subject to teen suicide and to adult alcoholism.

No one can read Ellen Herman's discerning book without gaining insight into the extent of suffering these assorted theories and treatments have produced in gay people themselves. The reader will come to understand, too, why gay activists by the 1960s, no longer able to bear the smugness of experts nor to contain their mounting anger at their abuses, finally rose up and challenged reigning orthodoxies about the "meaning" of homosexuality. It was the early gay liberationists themselves—many of whom had *not* bought into the notion that they were "sick"—who created the countermodels and political pressure groups that helped to change psychiatric attitudes.

Once gay people began to think of *themselves* as experts on their own lives, the modern gay/lesbian political movement flowered—and the misrule of the psychiatric homophobes drew to a close. Which is not to say, Herman cautions us, that the struggle against oppression has been entirely won. Some psychologists—like Joseph Nicolosi—continue to advocate "cures" for homosexuality, and in some places psychiatric institutionalization, particularly for adolescents, continues to be practiced.

On balance, as Herman puts it, "large numbers of experts now see homosexuality as a viable and healthy orientation and blame many of the problems associated with gay and lesbian life on antigay prejudice and social policy, rather than on homosexuality itself." But as she also warns, "More than 20 years after Stonewall, many psychological experts have not yet adjusted." The struggle for acceptance is ongoing—and Ellen Herman's book eloquently demonstrates why.

1

Getting to Normal

Am I normal? For gay men and lesbians in modern America, this seemingly simple question has been anything but simple. Sometimes it has provoked waves of self-loathing; sometimes it has inspired hopes of self-acceptance. Whether homosexuality is considered "normal" or "abnormal," "healthy" or "sick" has made a profound difference in how gay people feel about themselves and one another. And how gay people feel has altered what they think and how they behave. The difference between normal and abnormal has been the difference between secrecy and openness. It has been the difference between hiding in shame and marching with pride.

"If I could be 'normal,'" one gay man from Chicago wrote sadly to Ann Landers not long ago, "I would grab that option in a heartbeat." When he used the word "normal," he was referring to a favorable state of emotional, mental, and sexual well-being associated with heterosexuality. As a goal, normality is culturally mandated. It is not personal. Individuals do not choose to be normal or abnormal in the same way they develop tastes for one type of food or another. During the past century, being accepted as normal has evolved into the equivalent of being good, being right, or even being admirable. Americans have come to believe that achieving normality (as the culture currently defines it) is necessary in order to be a psychologically healthy person, a happy human being, and a contributing member of society. By the same token, being abnormal is feared and avoided at all costs, as if it was exactly the same as being miserable and living in disgrace.

During the early history of the United States, religion offered masses of people rules for daily living and served as a yardstick by which to measure their successes and failures. Today, psychology is as or more likely than religious creed to guide the attitudes and behaviors of Americans. Being emotionally and mentally normal is among the dominant cultural ideals of America in the late 20th century, and we actively strive for it as children and adults, as members of families, as friends, and as lovers. Normality—and this most certainly includes heterosexuality—may be the most compelling ethical imperative of our time. It is something we *should* be.

Throughout the 20th century, psychological experts have been normality's judges, gatekeepers, and manufacturers. In psychiatry, psychology, social work, and counseling, scientists and "helping professionals" have defined normality, devised techniques for diagnosing deviations from it, and offered therapeutic means of *becoming* normal for those who were not lucky enough to start out that way or who managed to veer off course at some point in their lives.

Because normality encompasses the territory of love and sexuality, psychological experts have had an especially powerful impact on the social experience of gay and lesbian Americans. At times when homosexuality was rarely, if ever, discussed in polite company, these were the experts most likely to meet, study, and "help" gay men and lesbians. One of the results was that gay men and lesbians have often recognized themselves for the first time in clinical casebooks or in weighty mental health references under the letter *H*. Although they

Is he normal? In 1993, with his election as alderman for the city of Albany, New York, Keith St. John became the first openly gay black elected official in the United States.

almost always discovered that their feelings were considered "sick" or "deviant," the literature of psychological expertise at least confirmed that homosexuals existed, and this could be welcome news to a young person or an adult suffering alone and in silence. Psychological experts were also the people who brought information about homosexuality to the attention of the general public. What caused homosexuality? How widespread was it? Could it be prevented? Was there a cure? Publicity about homosexuality and visibility for homosexuals almost always went hand in hand.

The consistent attention psychological experts paid to homosexuality, along with their growing authority in our recent history, has left marks on gay identity and community life. The view that homosexuality is a psychological "condition," for example, has shaped the lives of all gay men and lesbians in the United States today. Even though most of us (like most Americans) have never been research subjects in psychological experiments, patients in psychiatric hospitals, or clients in psychotherapy, psychological literature on homosexuality is pretty easy to find, and sometimes it is the only available information. More than any other group of experts in recent years, therefore, psychological experts have affected the lives of gay men and lesbians. Their power is not difficult to understand: psychological experts can either uphold or challenge the conventional belief that heterosexuality is normal and homosexuality is not. During the time period covered by this book, they have done both.

They have often used their power as experts to confuse science with prejudice, not that it was always easy to tell the difference. They have endorsed heterosexual ideals and classified gay experience as loveless, emotionally disturbed, sexually perverted, and probably the result of a personality disorder with roots in faulty childhood development. In 1956, for example, psychoanalyst Edmund Bergler wrote, "I have no bias against homosexuality; for me they are sick people requiring medical help. . . . Still, though I have no bias, if I were asked what kind of person the homosexual is, I would say: 'Homosexuals are essentially disagreeable people, regardless of their pleasant or unpleasant character.'" At times when such attitudes were prevalent, it is little wonder that gay people absorbed the view that they were mentally ill, morally disgraceful, and destined to live empty lives likely to end in suicide. Nor is it surprising that, in later years, views such as Bergler's would make psychology and psychiatry virtually synonymous with antihomosexual propaganda.

But the experts have not always expressed views like Bergler's. Also in 1956, Dr. Charles Berg insisted that "homosexuality is not a disease,

Revelers proclaim their individuality at the 1992 Wigstock celebration in Tompkins Square Park in New York City. Such displays might indeed strike some onlookers as out of the norm, but so are many varieties of heterosexual behavior.

nor even a clinical entity, it is nothing more than a particular form of expression of a psychic state which is common to all living creatures." Experts like Berg have been advocates for gay men and lesbians. By championing the idea that homosexuality is a benign example of the sexual diversity and potential found in nature—rather than a sickness

Is she normal? New York City police officer Fran de Benedictis is the secretary of the Gay Officers Action League (GOAL), an organization for gay and lesbian members of the New York City Police Department. In the summer of 1994, when this picture was taken, GOAL had a membership of approximately 1,000 officers. "We thought, 'Let's show people how normal we really are,'" said officer Jim Andruskewicz, another member of the organization.

in need of treatment or cure—psychological experts have advanced an agenda of openness, respect, and toleration. They have, in other words, brought homosexuality closer to normal.

Whether the experts supported homophobia or worked against it, their theories and research have significantly shaped social and cultural views of homosexuality in modern America. Because gay men and lesbians have always understood that their own self-esteem was tied to the fate of these experts, campaigns to recruit experts to the cause of homosexual rights or denounce them as enemies of the gay community have been vigorous and frequent in recent gay and lesbian history, from those launched by the Mattachine Society of the 1950s to those directed by the National Gay and Lesbian Task Force today. Equally important, however, have been efforts by gay men and lesbians to escape the clutches of experts, reject the confining logic of psychological normality, and define themselves on their own terms. For many participants in the 1969 Stonewall riots, and for many young gay people today, questions about the causes of homosexuality seem stupid and irrelevant in comparison to questions about the causes of homophobia. Being normal is not the point; living a happy, "queer" life is.

This book describes the love–hate relationship between gay people and psychological experts, who have sometimes treated one another like enemies and sometimes behaved like best friends. It describes how they have struggled for decades over how homosexuality should be defined. Although they sometimes argued about technical-sounding things such as the research design of sexological studies and the wording of medical diagnoses, normality was never a purely technical matter. It did not concern scientists and physicians alone, and the results reached far beyond isolated ivory towers and dusty medical books. The real battle was always about how the larger culture would view homosexuality, how American society would treat its gay and lesbian citizens, and how gay men and lesbians would feel about themselves.

This book focuses primarily on the 50 years since World War II. During this era, psychological experts have become very prominent members of American society. Their research and theories, respected as "scientific" and "objective," have been widely discussed by policy-

The consequences of stigmatizing any group as other, lesser, inferior, or abnormal can be profound. Newly elected to San Francisco's board of supervisors, openly gay Harvey Milk greets the press in front of his camera shop in November 1977. Over his left shoulder hangs a handwritten sign informing the gay community of a recent incident of gaybashing that resulted in the murder of a young gay man. About a year later, Milk himself was murdered in city hall by a homophobic former city supervisor.

makers and ordinary citizens alike. Growing public demand for their advice has dramatically increased the market for everything from psychotherapy to talk shows on radio and television. During this same period, gay men and lesbians have also become a much more visible and powerful social group. World War II brought thousands of gay men and lesbians into contact with one another and, after the war, they formed communities in America's urban centers. During the 1950s and 1960s, a tiny but vocal minority campaigned for toleration and respect in homophile organizations like the Mattachine Society and Daughters of Bilitis. After the Stonewall riots in June 1969, when patrons at a Greenwich Village bar fought back against a routine police raid, gay Americans launched a mass freedom movement that has been growing ever since. That movement has started to change the way psychological experts think about homosexuality, just as surely as psychology and psychiatry have shaped the way gay men and lesbians in modern America have always felt.

2

Doctors Discover the Homosexual

The Anglo-Irish dramatist, wit, and critic Oscar Wilde is perhaps the most famous martyr to the societal view that regarded homosexuality as criminal behavior. Wilde scandalized English society in the 1890s with the flamboyant openness of his lifestyle and was imprisoned for engaging in homosexual relations.

IT IS SAFE TO assume that men have had sex with other men and women with women throughout all of history, but until approximately one century ago, homosexuality was understood mainly as wicked behavior—not a "condition" or a state of being. Without a stiff moral backbone, almost any man or woman could be tempted into homosexual behavior, or so it was thought. Their behavior might have been depraved and shameful, but it was probably also temporary. Clergy and police were therefore much more likely than psychological experts to be interested in homosexuality, which was considered a sin, a vice, or a crime.

*The inversion theory of homo-
sexuality, which proposed that
gay men and lesbians possessed
the psychological makeup of the
opposite biological sex, has long
since been discredited.*

In the late 19th century, psychiatrists turned homosexuality into a disease. Trying hard to distinguish themselves from other medical specialists who studied the anatomy and chemistry of the human body, psychiatrists began to circulate an intriguing idea about homosexuality in the literature of medicine and psychology. What if homosexuals were unique *personalities,* different than heterosexuals not only in their behavior but in their hearts and minds?

The first case study of a homosexual published in the United States appeared in 1879, and it treated its subject as brand-new, as if homosexuality had never existed before. The view of homosexuals as almost a different species, and of homosexuality as a disordered state of being, was striking. In today's terminology, the medical experts had discovered that "having sex" was not the same thing as "sexual orientation" or "sexual preference." The former was about what a person *did*. The latter was about who a person *was*.

"Sexual invert" was the term many experts used during this period to refer to the newly discovered homosexual person. It indicated that homosexuality was conceptualized as an inversion—a reversal—of gender identity: "a woman is physically a woman and psychologically a man and, on the other hand, a man is physically a man and psychologically a woman." Inversion explains why so much attention was devoted to finding effeminate passivity in men and mannish aggressiveness in women. For women who supposedly wanted to be men and for men who wanted to be women, homosexual relationships were, the experts concluded, a pathetic effort to come as close as possible to normal heterosexuality.

The discovery of "sexual inversion" could not even begin to explain why so many feminine women and masculine men were also sexually attracted to people of the same sex. In fact, it made them invisible. But for some homosexuals at least, the theory was still welcome. It helped them to make sense out of their feelings and experiences and offered comfort as a result. "I just concluded that I had . . . a dash of the masculine," Frances Wilder wrote in 1915. As a feminist who had decided that sexual abstinence was the most positive choice for women, Wilder found herself tortured by a "strong desire to caress & fondle" a female friend. "I have been told more than once that I have a masculine mind," she added by way of explanation. Twenty years later, a lesbian subject in a study conducted by the Committee for the Study of Sex Variants in New York expressed similar views. "I can look at a woman exactly as a man does," Alberta I. informed psychiatrist George Henry. "I feel so much like a man that I don't understand how a woman falls in love with a woman."

While physicians firmly believed that their scientific outlook was a compassionate advance over older ideas that sharply condemned homosexual beastliness and abomination, those older ideas did not immediately disappear. Medical reports frequently mixed disapproval with fascination and caring with judgment. In 1884, according to Dr. George F. Shrady,

> The physician learns . . . and finds . . . far down beneath the surface of ordinary social life, currents of human passion and action that would shock and sicken the mind not accustomed to think everything pertaining to living creatures worthy of study. Science has indeed discovered that, amid the lowest forms of bestiality and sensuousness exhibited by debased men, there are phenomena which are truly pathological and which deserve the considerate attention and help of the physician.

Some homosexual men and women agreed that enlightened medical help and attention would improve their lives. In the 1890s, when 17-year-old Ralph Lind shared his worries about his sinful sexual nature with his minister, he was advised to seek medical assistance. But the first physician Lind consulted instructed him to turn his erotic attention to women and left it at that. "Like most physicians in 1890," Lind wrote later, "he did not understand the deepseated character of my perversion." After a series of other doctors did nothing but offer drugs that eliminated his sexual drive, Lind began a course of study on his own and read everything he could find about homosexuality at the New York Academy of Medicine. Finally, he wrote an account of his own life, *Autobiography of an Androgyne,* in hopes of reaching doctors, and other patients like himself, with the message that homosexuality could not, and should not, be changed.

But at the turn of the century, Lind's view—the new view—of homosexuals as a type was not yet widespread. Nor did everyone share the doctors' view that homosexuality was "morbid" and "pathological." Doctors frequently wrote about their frustration that most homosexuals at the time had "no occasion to go to a physician; they enjoy their abnormal life." Further, some men and women saw no reason to treat their same-sex love affairs as evidence that they were "abnormal" homosexuals. For example, during a navy investigation of homosexuality among sailors at the Newport, Rhode Island, Naval Training Station in 1919, a straight-identified man named Rogers argued that homosexual activity did not make him a homosexual, even though he knew men who were. "I got in their company. I don't know why; but

I used to go out with them. . . . This is something that I never did until I came in the Navy."

Especially in working-class communities, terms based on sexual practices or gender roles—such as "queers," "fairies," "dykes," and "bull daggers"—remained as or more common than "invert" well into the 20th century. In big cities such as New York, where vibrant gay communities thrived, many homosexuals insisted that their love and sex lives were perfectly normal and very enjoyable. In the 1930s, Kathleen M. explained,

> When Mother told me about homosexuality she told me it was abnormal, that there was no satisfaction and that the result was an empty life. I disagree. I don't care what people think and I avoid people who ask personal questions. My personal life is my own affair. Since we have been living together our lives are fuller and happier.

For many men and women, homosexuality was still about what they did and not who they were, no matter what the experts said.

3

Freud's Revolution

THE DOCTOR WHOSE CURIOSITY about human sexuality was most important at the turn of the century was certainly Sigmund Freud, a Viennese physician born in 1856. Freud is known as the founder of psychoanalysis, which is both a psychological theory and a type of therapeutic treatment. Because Freud placed sexuality at the center of his theory, his ideas were often greeted with horror and ridicule at a time when Victorian sensibilities still made sex unmentionable, and even unthinkable, in polite company. For example, controversy surrounded Freud's claim that infants and young children were pleasure-seeking creatures—he called them "polymorphously perverse"—who matured through sequential stages of psychosexual development, a radical departure from a vision of childhood as a pure and asexual time. Further, psychoanalysis assumed that erotic and incestuous feelings too

The psychoanalytic theories of Sigmund Freud emphasized the influence of unconscious motivations and sexuality on human behavior.

shocking to remember were buried (or "repressed") in the unconscious, where they became a major cause of human suffering and mental anguish. For Freud, human sexuality was always intricate and usually unpredictable. Its shape and direction depended upon a complicated relationship between genetic inheritance and cultural forces subject to social choice. He was a scientist, but he was also a moralist.

Freud hypothesized that all people were born with a constitutional capacity for bisexuality. It was natural, Freud thought, for both males and females to tend toward aggression and passivity, masculinity and femininity, and all children moved through a homosexual phase on their way to becoming heterosexual. None of these natural endowments for a range of gender and sexual identities ever disappeared entirely, according to Freud. They were simply repressed in the course of a developmental process whose end point was heterosexuality.

Even more than in Europe, people in America were so scandalized by Freud's openness about sexual matters that it was not unusual for everything else about his thought to be ignored. During the first two decades of the 20th century, when psychoanalysis was first introduced into American culture, reform movements dedicated to eliminating prostitution and other sexual vices were flourishing. Many well-educated citizens were determined to achieve "social purity," a vision that equated social progress with strict marital monogamy, rigid gender distinctions, and numerous sexual prohibitions. Ironically, Freud's theory spread more rapidly in America than it did in Europe. When he visited America in 1909, Freud attracted a group of devoted followers who tirelessly promoted psychoanalysis within the medical profession. Even more important, Freud's ideas about mental healing found a welcome home in a country where mind cure, hypnosis, and suggestion were already popular fads.

Because it challenged sexual silence in the name of science, Freudian psychology was crucial to changing cultural views about sexuality in general and homosexuality in particular. "Sexual morality as society— and at its most extreme, American society—defines it, seems very despicable to me," Freud candidly wrote to an American colleague. "I stand for a much freer sexual life." Freud's revolution made it possible

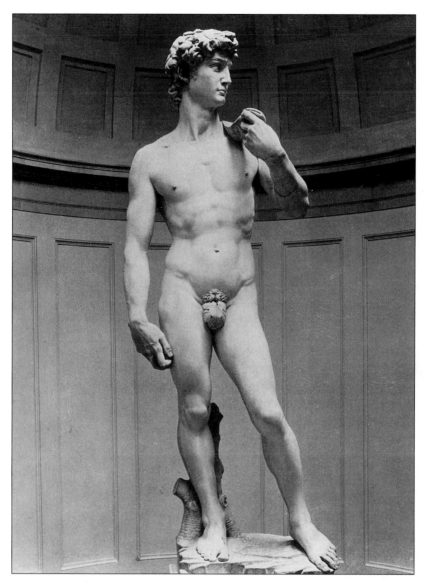

Michelangelo's David is regarded as one of the absolute masterpieces of Western civilization. Freud often cited Michelangelo as an example that homosexuality was not necessarily debilitating or crippling. "It is one of the obvious injustices of social life," Freud wrote, "that the standards of culture should demand the same behavior in sexual life from everyone."

not only to speak out loud about sexual feelings and behaviors but to imagine changing them as well.

Even so, Freud's opinions about homosexuality were confusing. On the one hand, he wrote admiringly about great homosexuals such as Italian artists Michelangelo and Leonardo da Vinci, implying that homosexuality (at least among men) was compatible with normal mental life, even creative genius! On the other hand, he viewed procreation as an inescapable biological necessity and the aim of normal sexuality. "One of the tasks implicit in object choice," Freud wrote, "is that it should find its way to the opposite sex." In comparison, homosexuality seemed second best, surely a sharp detour from the important goal of producing children through heterosexual bonds.

Freud's most famous statement about homosexuality appeared in a letter he wrote to an American woman in 1935, after she contacted him for advice about her son. He responded,

> I gather from your letter that your son is a homosexual. I am most impressed by the fact that you do not mention this term yourself in your information about him. May I question you, why you avoid it? Homosexuality is assuredly no advantage but it is nothing to be ashamed of, no vice, no degradation, it cannot be classified as an illness; we consider it to be a variation of the sexual function produced by a certain arrest of sexual development. Many highly respectable individuals of ancient and modern times have been homosexuals, several of the greatest men among them (Plato, Michelangelo, Leonardo da Vinci, etc.). It is a great injustice to persecute homosexuality as a crime, and cruelty too.

Not an illness, yet still the result of an "arrest of sexual development." What are we to make of this? Ever since Freud's death, psychoanalysts have been debating this very question. While it seems reasonable to conclude that his views were vague enough to support different answers to the question of whether homosexuality was "normal" or "abnormal," "sick" or "healthy," there was never any doubt about his position on the public status of homosexuality. In contrast to many of his colleagues, Freud did not believe that homosexuals should be barred from membership in psychoanalytic societies. And in 1930, Freud signed a statement advocating that homosexuality be removed from the criminal laws of Germany and Austria. His support for legal reform at this early date made him a gay rights pioneer of sorts.

"It is not for psychoanalysis to solve the problem of homosexuality," Freud wrote in 1920. "To undertake to convert a fully developed homosexual into a heterosexual is not much more promising than to do the reverse." For him, psychoanalysis might clarify the psychological origins of homosexuality but could never hope to "cure" it. Many of the doctors and therapists who later elaborated upon his theories about homosexuality—and offered analytic therapy to suffering gay men and women—did not share this view, as we shall see.

4

The Sexy War

FREUD DIED IN 1939, the same year that Hitler invaded Poland and World War II began in Europe. Two years later, after the bombing of Pearl Harbor by the Japanese, the United States entered the war.

The massive wartime mobilization involved just about everyone. For millions of Americans, life would never be the same again. Women who had never before worked for wages, or who had only worked in "feminine" jobs as secretaries and domestic servants, spent the war years building airplanes and driving trucks. Even children pitched in, collecting thousands of tons of old newspapers, tin cans, and rubber to aid the war effort. Masses of poor Americans, black and white, surged out of the rural South and into northern cities, where the promise of jobs in war industries signaled a brighter future. Lesbians and gay men were also on the move. Jim Kepner, who came out during the war years, remembered that the military emer-

Gay veterans of World War II demonstrate in front of the White House as part of the March on Washington for Lesbian and Gay Rights in April 1993.

gency "brought a lot more people from the hinterlands out into conditions where they weren't living in small towns, where they were freer, where they met other people and, male and female, got into close, same-sex relationships and developed friendships." Ex-army chaplain George Buse had similar perceptions about that period: "Even though we were totally 'closeted' then, at least there was a certain perception that we weren't geographically isolated."

Psychological experts were among the very first to volunteer for the war effort. Since the millions of soldiers (mostly men, but there were some women, too) flooding into the military were the country's critical first line of defense, they reasoned, the military needed a comprehensive, top-notch program of psychiatric screening, psychological testing, and clinical treatment. Experts promised that every single recruit would be inspected for signs of mental trouble before induction in order to weed out unstable individuals who were likely to be a drain on the military. And once in the military, soldiers would be carefully watched under conditions of stress and treated for mental anguish when they snapped.

President Franklin Roosevelt was worried about alarming predictions that the financial costs of the war's mental casualties might be extremely high. So he gave his blessing to the psychiatric planners, who promised to save the country money, and psychological screening became part of the 1940 Selective Service Act, which instituted the draft. Eventually, a total of 2.5 million soldiers were rejected or discharged from the military for "neuropsychiatric" reasons. No other pretext for military rejection came remotely close to this figure. Of the men who passed their initial exam, 163,000 were later given "dishonorable" discharges for reasons including psychopathic personality, drug addiction, alcoholism, and homosexuality. So shocking did the public find these rejection and discharge rates that in the fall of 1943 the military censored information about its soldiers' mental health, but secrets about so many men could not be kept for long. World War II gave military officials and the general public convincing evidence that emotional disturbance was so rampant among American men that it qualified as a threat to national security.

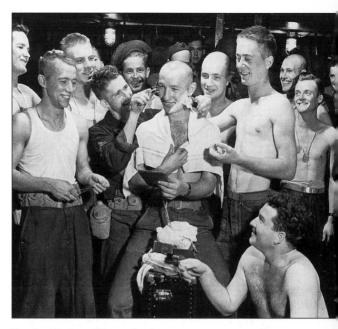

An American GI gets a shave and a haircut from his comrades-in-arms aboard a troop ship bound for Australia in the early months of World War II. The American public has always had a difficult time believing that some of its fighting men and women are gay or lesbian.

Prior to World War II, the U.S. military had never systematically tried to prevent homosexuals from entering the service. Even at the beginning of World War II, local draft boards were not instructed to screen out homosexuals, who were not initially included in the military's "categories of handicap" or even in its list of psychiatric "deviations." The first director of the military screening program, Harry Stack Sullivan, was probably responsible for this. A Freudian psychiatrist and director of the prestigious William Alanson White Foundation, Sullivan described himself as a "mild-looking bachelor." For almost 22 years, he lived with a longtime companion, Jimmie, and he was almost certainly gay himself, though very few people who knew it were willing to admit as much.

By May 1941, the army surgeon general had declared that "homosexual proclivities" were a disqualifying "deviation" and a sufficient reason to reject an inductee from military service. But how exactly were the gatekeepers supposed to detect homosexuality? One early suggestion was to ask men to undress and keep them naked during their entire psychiatric examination. Another was to ask them point-blank whether they had homosexual feelings or at least inquire: "Do you like girls?" Showing discomfort about being naked, or showing embarrassment when describing sexual experiences, were considered clues about the potential for homosexuality. But the surest signs—feminine bodily characteristics and effeminate dress or behavior—had to do with violating gender norms, a holdover from the theory of "sexual inversion" earlier in the century.

Interestingly, women who strayed from their proper roles were not generally treated with the same suspicion. "Women showing a masculine manner may be perfectly normal sexually and excellent military material," advised Marine Corps examiners. Even when they were not "perfectly normal sexually," the presence of lesbian soldiers did not seem to pose as great a threat. "A lot of the commanding officers knew what the score was," recalled a former member of the Women's Auxiliary Army Corps (WAAC). "Sometimes we would get these guys, these straight guys with a couple of bars or even a star, and ask them point–blank—who are the best women in the company—and they'd say most of them were dykes."

As military psychiatrists refined their methods of detection, they had to deal with an unanticipated problem. What would happen if lots of men claimed to be homosexual in order to get out of the service alive or even avoid it altogether?

As it turned out, such fears proved largely groundless. Few heterosexuals were willing to endure the shame of being considered homosexual, and besides, there were easier ways to avoid military service than pretending to be homosexual. Of the millions of young men, and thousands of young women, who had to talk to psychiatrists before induction, few gay men or lesbians voluntarily declared their homosexuality either. "I remember being very nervous about them asking me if I had any homosexual feelings or attitude," recalled Phyllis Arby, a lesbian WAAC. "I just smiled and was sweet and feminine!" Charles Rowland, from Phoenix, remembered thinking: "We were not about to be deprived of the privilege of serving our country in a time of great national emergency by virtue of some stupid regulation about being gay."

In spite of the new policy that declared homosexuals unsuitable for military service, and in spite of new procedures designed to help ferret them out, only a handful of soldiers and sailors (fewer than 5,000) were actually rejected in advance from the World War II military for being homosexual. Apparently unable to identify homosexuals at the point of induction, psychological experts soon turned their efforts in a new direction. What should be done about homosexuals who were "found out" after they had already entered the military?

Psychological experts had a lot to say on this question. For the most part, they argued that homosexuals were sick and should be treated with understanding, not punishment. Before World War II, service members accused of homosexuality were subject to court-martial for the crime of sodomy, and if they were found guilty, they could be sentenced to long prison terms. During World War II, psychiatric research and practice led to major reforms. Homosexuality was reformulated as a serious psychological disturbance requiring diagnosis and professional clinical treatment. It was increasingly seen in Freudian terms, as a problem of faulty psychosexual development. As they had done with the screening program, experts initially played upon financial concerns to achieve their aim of substituting a psychiatric approach for a penal one. "Confinement is not a cure for sexual perversion," reported one team of military psychiatrists in 1942. Prison "will not even act as an effective deterrent. . . . The government assumes the enormous expense of caring for these men for long periods of time with no possible return from the investment."

Under the new regime of military psychiatry, homosexuality was still not officially compatible with military service, but instead of being sent to military prisons, gay men and lesbians who were caught were likely to find themselves in psychotherapy or assigned to mental wards in military hospitals. This is exactly where Marvin Liebman ended up, after his personal letters were censored and he was harshly interrogated by his commanding officer, who accused him of being a "cocksucker." Liebman remembers feeling like an outcast, and he lied about his sexual orientation from that moment until he finally came out of the closet at age 67. Being kicked out of the military was, for Liebman, "the most devastating experience of my life." For the psychological experts, the military's new frame of reference was evidence of definite progress. "The crude methods of the past have given way to more humane and satisfactory handling of the problems of the homosexual," the *Journal of the American Medical Association* pointed out with pride. "No longer is it necessary to subject cases that are so definitely in the medical field to the routine of military court-martial."

Gay men and lesbians, however, often paid a high price for this new "enlightenment," as Marvin Liebman discovered. Even if they followed the military's advice and voluntarily talked over their feelings with the unit physician or chaplain, they might find their confidentiality violated and themselves kicked out of the service for honestly revealing their sexual preference. It was true that instead of criminal records, they were given medical discharges, but the "undesirable" label stamped on their paperwork was a stigma that separated homosexuals (and everyone who fell under the umbrella of mental illness) from "normal" soldiers. To be wounded in the course of performing military duty was honorable. To be homosexual was not. Altogether, 4,000 sailors and 5,000 soldiers

American sailors grab some shut-eye onboard a battleship in the Pacific theater during World War II. Homophobes have consistently cited the close proximity in which soldiers live and work as an argument against admitting homosexuals to the military.

were hospitalized and discharged under the new system of "humane" psychiatric treatment in World War II, and the fact of their homosexuality was permanently recorded in their record of military service. In comparison, only a few hundred individuals had been court-martialed in the years between the two world wars.

By the time World War II ended, psychiatric authority over the definition and treatment of homosexuality had expanded significantly. Their screening, treatment, and discharge efforts had all brought experts into contact with many gay men and lesbians and stimulated their curiosity about homosexuality. But there was still a great deal of disagreement about exactly what caused homosexuality in the first place and how psychological experts should identify and treat it. Was it always a symptom of arrested psychological development, as Freud had suggested, or could it be a harmless sexual variation in people who were otherwise well-adjusted and happy? Harsh and sex-segregated conditions, such as those facing service members in basic training and combat, led some experts to observe that "normal" men might even turn to homosexuality temporarily, with little or no harmful effect. Perhaps many more kinds of homosexuals existed than anyone had previously believed.

During the war years, at least 15 studies of male homosexuality were published by military psychiatrists, based on more than 2,000 male subjects. (None were published about lesbians and only a few about the sexual behavior of heterosexual soldiers.) In their zeal to improve diagnostic and clinical techniques, psychiatrists administered psychological tests (such as the Rorschach inkblot), explored subjects' family backgrounds and sexual histories, took their urine, and examined their bodies in great detail. Their aim was to compile an accurate picture of the homosexual personality and reveal its causes. To their amazement, they often found that such a "typical" picture did not exist.

Psychological research inadvertently helped to destroy old stereotypes and changed the minds of some experts. "Overt homosexuality occurs in a heterogeneous group of individuals," was the conclusion of many of the wartime studies. Even the effeminate traits that most psychiatrists thought so characteristic of male homosexuals—sissiness, high-pitched voices, and unusual closeness to their mothers—were not reliable indicators. Nor did their studies prove that gay men were always poor soldiers or likely to undermine the morale of their heterosexual peers, two important foundations of the military's antihomosexual policy. Shocked to discover that homosexuals could be just as "normal" as anyone else, some experts bent rules to protect their gay patients from the worst consequences of exposure. Although they represented a tiny minority, these psychological experts became advocates of toleration and respect long before a mass movement for gay rights became visible. In many ways, their efforts paved the way for homophile organizations such as the Mattachine Society and Daughters of Bilitis (DOB) in the years after the war.

So far as homosexuality is concerned, the most important thing about the World War II experience is that homosexuals and psychological experts came into much greater contact with one another than they had in the past. For the experts, the experience was a good one in every way. It helped to advance their position in the military hierarchy and extend their authority over more people and more types of abnormality than ever before. It is not really surprising that they believed future efforts to study and help homosexuals would work to their own, as well as their patients', advantage.

For gay men and lesbians, the experience was not quite as rosy. That psychiatrists and psychologists took steps to understand homosexuality in psychological terms *was* an advance over a purely punitive system, and it was also obvious that liberal-minded psychological experts were largely responsible for this shift, even though Freud had expressed toleration and sympathy for the legal rights of homosexuals 15 years before the end of World War II. On the other hand, because the close attention the experts paid to homosexuality was founded first and foremost on the desire to eliminate homosexuals from the military, their purpose was hardly friendly. The profile of homosexuality as an emotional disease was not designed to make gay men and lesbians feel more comfortable with themselves. In accepting the experts' view of homosexuality as a mental and emotional disability—and even many of the most militant gay men and lesbians did—they were gambling that

One of the effects that World War II had on American society was to alter prevailing attitudes regarding women's capabilities and their proper role in the workplace. With so many men called to military service, women were expected to step forward and take a place in the front lines of the nation's wartime industrial effort, like these four grandmothers who took jobs with the Federal Ship Building and Drydock Company.

psychological authority was more likely to chip away at ignorance and bigotry than to stigmatize homosexuality further or eliminate it entirely through "cures."

In the end, helping professionals who were sworn to preserve human welfare appeared to be more concerned with upholding military policy than with aiding their patients. Military service in World War II proved to be a turning point in the lives of many gay men and lesbians, as the fledgling urban gay communities of the postwar years were built on the foundations of wartime friendships, social networks, and geographic mobility among soldiers and civilians alike. They had learned that psychological experts were powerful allies if you could get them on your side. But they also knew that these experts usually were not.

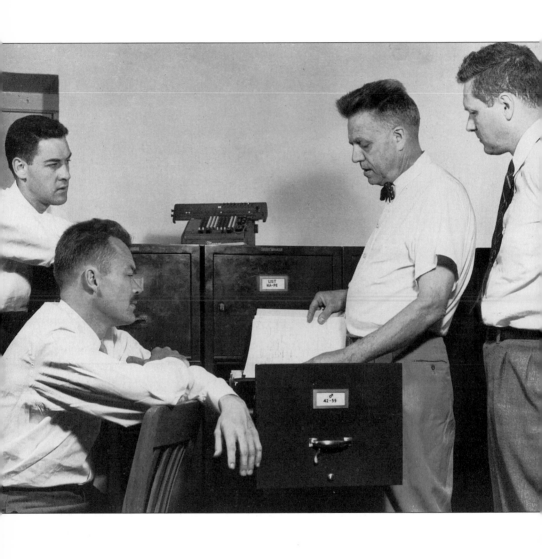

5

The Science of Sex

THE FIRST, MOST POWERFUL ally to emerge in the years after World War II, Alfred Kinsey was in many ways an unlikely friend of the gay and lesbian community.

A professor of zoology at Indiana University, Kinsey spent years studying gall wasps (he had a personal collection of more than 4 million) before turning his attention to human sexual behavior. Though the subject of Kinsey's research may have changed dramatically in 1939, his approach did not. Inspired by scientific ideals and the model of objective research, Kinsey was convinced that adding to the limited store of knowledge about sexuality would serve not only to forge a legitimate new sexual science but to promote human welfare by providing people with factual, dispassionate information. His aim was "to accumulate an objectively determined body of facts about sex which strictly avoids social or moral interpretations of the facts." He was careful to note that "each person will want to make interpretations in accordance with his understanding of moral values and social signifi-

Behaviorist Alfred Kinsey's groundbreaking study of human sexual behavior was so controversial that only these four men were allowed access to the heavily guarded rooms at the University of Indiana where the data was stored. From left to right are Dr. Clyde Martin, Dr. Paul Gebhard, Kinsey, and Dr. Wardell Pomeroy.

cance; but that is not part of the scientific method, and indeed, scientists have no special capacities for making such evaluations."

The results of his sexological research, the famous Kinsey reports on male and female sexual behavior, were published in 1948 and 1953, respectively. Funded by the Rockefeller Foundation and sponsored by the National Research Council's Committee for Research in Problems of Sex (CRPS), they systematically reported the results of Kinsey's massive study, based on the sexual histories of literally thousands of Americans—college students, prisoners, white-collar and blue-collar workers, housewives, ministers, prostitutes, and mental patients—each one of whom answered 350–500 direct questions about their sexual tastes and experiences during two-hour-long interviews. Although the size and diversity of Kinsey's sample were unprecedented (all previous efforts to study sexual behavior scientifically had been based on single case studies or very small samples), all of his subjects were white. Deeply concerned about the statistical validity of his research, Kinsey worried that presenting conclusions based on the sexual histories of only small numbers of black men and women would undermine the scientific authority of his conclusions. Kinsey believed that if only the numbers were large enough, the scientific truth about sex could be discovered. His ultimate goal was to compile 100,000 sexual histories, but he died first, in 1956.

Kinsey counted and classified the "sexual outlets" of 5,300 men and 5,940 women according to six major sources of orgasm: masturbation, nocturnal emissions, heterosexual petting, heterosexual intercourse, homosexual relations, and sex with animals. Then he placed his subjects on a seven-point scale (he called it "the heterosexual-homosexual balance") that ranged from exclusive heterosexuality at one end to exclusive homosexuality at the other. (The scale was designed to reflect subjects' reports about their physical responses and emotional attachments.) Unlike Freud and so many of the psychological experts who had studied homosexuality during World War II, Kinsey did not search for causes or cures. What made people homosexual (or heterosexual, for that matter) was not the point, nor did questions of identity attract his interest. For Kinsey, sexuality was a straightforward physical and biological reality for human beings. Everyone, he believed, had the capacity for homosexual behavior. "The homosexual has been a significant part of human sexual activity ever since the dawn of history," Kinsey explained, "primarily because it is an expression of capacities that are basic to the human animal." Documenting what people did sexually—not what they said about who they were or what they believed to be right—was Kinsey's goal.

Because he illustrated that actual sexual practice diverged sharply from accepted sexual morality, Kinsey's work was extremely controversial. People did a lot of unconventional things, sexually speaking, placing their behavior in direct conflict with a dominant cultural ideology that pronounced monogamous heterosexuality the only natural form of sexual expression and certainly the only permissible one. For instance, Kinsey's study showed that a significant number of Americans—26 percent of women and 50 percent of men—had extramarital affairs. Less than half of all the orgasms men reported to Kinsey were the result of sexual intercourse with their wives, which meant that more than half were the result of socially despised activities, some of them defined as crimes. Kinsey also documented that masturbation was all but universal and, most originally, that class status (whether "upper level" or "lower level") shaped sexual experiences and attitudes rather directly.

Nothing Kinsey revealed was more shocking, though, than what he uncovered about the prevalence of homosexuality in America. "The data in the present study indicate that at least 37 per cent of the male population has some homosexual experience between the beginning of adolescence and old age," he calmly wrote in *Sexual Behavior in the Human Male*. Among women, Kinsey found that 28 percent had erotic responses to other women by the age of 45; 19 percent had some type of lesbian sexual contact by age 40. Kinsey estimated that exclusive homosexuality accounted for 10 percent of the entire U.S. population—somewhere around 20 million people—a figure far higher than any previous calculation.

Even before the final results were in, Kinsey's willingness to place despised and abnormal sexualities, especially bestiality and homosexuality, on a par with normal heterosexuality as sexual outlets made his research study a lightning rod for public controversy. One high school teacher, for example, lost his job simply for helping Kinsey to line up interviews in the city where he lived. Because Kinsey's data challenged accepted ideas about what was sexually normal, intense curiosity greeted each of the reports upon publication, and they became instant best-sellers.

Outrage was a common reaction as well. Prominent individuals were offended. The president of Princeton University, Harold W. Dodds, requested a meeting with officials at the Rockefeller Foundation to express his displeasure, and the flow of money from the CRPS to Kinsey was eventually cut off. Congressional representative Louis Heller of Brooklyn tried to prevent *Sexual Behavior in the Human Female* from being sent through the mails because, he raged, Kinsey was "hurling the insult of the century" at innocent women and adding to "the depravity of a whole generation, to the loss of faith in human dignity . . . to the spread of juvenile delinquency, and to the misunderstanding and confusion about sex." The American Medical Association publicly scolded Kinsey for provoking "a wave of sex hysteria" in 1954, and psychoanalyst Edmund Bergler denounced Kinsey's books as "statistical fairy tales" designed "to sell the public and its lawmakers the idea that perversion is completely normal." Bergler insisted bitterly that "Kinsey's conclusions provide homosexuals with an 'irrefutable,' 'statistical,' and 'scientific' argument enabling them to maintain and spread their perversion without conscious guilt. Both male and female homosexuals have taken Kinsey for a ride."

There was, however, no evidence that gay men and lesbians had any special influence with Kinsey, whose first and final commitment was to science. Still, gay men and lesbians went out of their way to aid his research, and Kinsey's staff was quick to acknowledge the important, behind-the-scenes contributions made by members of the gay community. Wardell Pomeroy, one of Kinsey's collaborators, explained:

Those who were bubbling over to tell us everything they could were usually homosexuals, particularly when they discovered by our use of homosexual argot that we knew all about the kind of lives they led. They would almost visibly expand with relief and eagerness to talk.

The final reports also brought hope and comfort to gay men and lesbians who had not been personally interviewed by the Kinsey team. Like other Americans, they treated the studies as confirmation that others lived and loved as they did. Kinsey's large-scale empirical approach undoubtedly encouraged all of his readers to weigh and measure their own sexual experiences against the unimpeachable standards of science. Kinsey's figures were hardly a green light to "spread perversion," as Bergler alleged, but they probably did provide gay men and lesbians with statistical reassurance that they were not alone. Homosexuals who read or heard about the Kinsey reports had good reason to conclude that they were members of a fairly substantial minority group. But since the 10 percent figure surprised so many people who were sure they had never met a gay man or lesbian, homosexuals could rest assured that they were also quite difficult to identify.

The text of the Kinsey reports was dry and uninteresting, and the charts and graphs were imposing, but the comfort of community and solidarity could be found in Kinsey's numbers. "Probably the reams of material written in passionate defense of the homophile have done less to further the cause of tolerance than Kinsey's single, detached statement that 37 per cent of the men and 19 per cent of the women whom he interviewed admitted having had overt homosexual relationships," one lesbian wrote appreciatively several years later. Kinsey may have placed his scientific work outside of religious morality and cultural values, but the fact that he made a spectrum of previously invisible human sexual behaviors visible to a large public served to affirm the variety of sexual desire and challenge the culture of sexual denial and repression. Thanks to Kinsey, homosexuality took a step closer to normal.

6

Expert
Enlightenment
and the Campaign
for Toleration

BACKLASH WAS THE PRICE of homosexuality's new visibility. During the early years of the cold war, memories of the wartime mental crises of American soldiers, sexual and otherwise, were still fresh. Although practical preoccupations with soldiers' mental health were not as pressing as they had been a few years earlier, experts were still determined to uncover the roots of widespread mental disturbance in men. The problem—in the experts' view—frequently turned out to be women's fault. Mothers, in particular, were blamed. "The mealy look of men today is the result of momism," wrote journalist Philip Wylie, and the term stuck. "Momism," throughout the postwar years, re-

51

ferred to the view that mothers were responsible for their sons' many problems, which, according to Wylie, included "hoodlumism, gang-sterism, labor strife, monopolistic thuggery, moral degeneration, civic corruption, smuggling, bribery, theft, murder, homosexuality, drunk-enness, financial depression, chaos and war."

Psychiatrist Edward Strecker, chair of the department of psychiatry at the University of Pennsylvania Medical School and a former presi-dent of the American Psychiatric Association, gave momism the psy-chiatric stamp of approval:

> Our war experiences—the alarming number of so-called "psychoneurotic" young Americans—point to and emphasize this threat to our survival. No one could view this huge test tube of man power, tried and found wanting, without realizing that an extremely important factor was the inability or unwillingness of the American mom and her surrogates to grant the boon of emotional emancipation during childhood.

Other experts glumly agreed that "women are the pivot around which much of the unhappiness of our day revolves, like a captive planet." Because mothers were producing a wave of emotionally confused children, including masculine girls and feminine boys, an-other "ghostly epidemic" of neurosis was sure to appear, threatening the country's moral fiber in a time of new national emergency: the cold war.

With danger lurking so close to home as well as in the arena of international political and ideological conflict, homosexuality became more than just a sensational subject of sexological investigations, such as the Kinsey reports. For several years, Senator Joseph McCarthy and the House Un-American Activities Committee conducted hearings around the country to investigate the subversive presence of Commu-nists in government, education, Hollywood, and elsewhere. According to McCarthy, godless communism and perverted sexuality were two sides of the same coin; the former polluted the mind, while the latter polluted the body. Consequently, homosexuality evolved into a public scandal of major proportions. Enemies were ferreted out by looking for any and all signs of dissent—sexual as well as political.

This logic implied that victory over the Communist threat involved preventing sexual seduction and betrayal by any means necessary. Simply teaching Americans to guard against ungodly socialistic doctrines would not be enough to win the cold war. In 1950, the U.S. Senate authorized an inquiry "to determine the extent of the employment of homosexuals and other sex perverts in Government; to consider reasons why their employment by the Government is undesirable; and to examine into the efficacy of the methods used in dealing with the problem." Well-known psychiatrists lined up to inform the senators that sexual deviation was a treatable, curable psychological illness. On the basis of this expert testimony, the investigating committee concluded that homosexuals "lack the emotional stability of normal persons." Not only did their devious characters and weak moral fiber make them unfit for responsibility and susceptible to blackmail, the report warned, but even a single "sex pervert in a Government agency tends to have a corrosive influence upon his fellow employees." The investigating subcommittee concluded that "there is no place in the United States Government for persons who violate the laws or the accepted standards of morality, or who otherwise bring disrepute to the Federal service by infamous or scandalous personal conduct."

President Truman subsequently signed an executive order barring homosexuals from government jobs, and a number of federal bureaucracies—from the post office to the military and the FBI—took the hint to step up their level of surveillance, harassment, and outright dismissal. Homosexuality was treated as a menace to national security and a danger that could slowly but surely destroy U.S. society from within, just as the forces of international communism were threatening it from without. In addition to discrimination in employment, same-sex dancing was banned and gay bars were routinely raided by police.

Joseph McCarthy himself was finally censured by the Senate in 1954 after he made the absurd claim that the U.S. military was a breeding ground for communism. But the damage had already been done to the lives and reputations of countless homosexual men and women. In an era without a powerful gay movement, it could not be reversed. The assumption that gay public servants posed special security risks outlasted

McCarthy himself by decades. In the late 1960s, gay activists were still asking sympathetic experts to "affirm that, in your professional judgment, it is indeed possible for a homosexual—including, specifically, those engaging in a continuing pattern of homosexual acts making up most or all of their sexual outlet—to be sufficiently emotionally stable to present no danger when entrusted with secret information." It was not until 1975 that the U.S. Civil Service Commission rejected McCarthy's policy and ruled that homosexuality could no longer disqualify men and women from working for the federal government.

It was in the hostile environment of McCarthyism that early homophile activists mounted their first concerted campaigns for toleration and respect. Organizations such as the Mattachine Society (which described itself as "a national educational and research agency on behalf of the sex-variant") began meeting secretly in 1950, and new members pledged that "no gay person coming into this world will ever again have to feel alone and unwanted and rejected." In exchange for helping researchers to locate subjects and publicize their findings, homophile activists hoped to reduce the stigma associated with homosexuality. "It seems incredible that people can be intelligent about certain things and so prejudiced about that," one lesbian commented. "I am particularly anxious to see some form of enlightenment on this subject. I think it is unpardonable to have such ignorance." With the record of World War II and the prestigious reputation of science in mind, it is not surprising that pioneering homophile organizations turned to psychological experts for sympathetic assistance. "Nobody would listen to us if we said we were OK," remembered Kay Lahusen, an activist with the Philadelphia chapter of Daughters of Bilitis. "Only if Dr. So-and-So persisted in his study and said we were OK would we really make progress."

By objectively demonstrating the prevalence of homosexuality historically and cross-culturally, early homophile activists hoped to secure their goals of respect and toleration through "EVOLUTION not REVOLUTION." According to Hal Call, a Mattachine activist in the early 1950s, this strategy appeared tame by the standards of the 1980s:

> We wanted to see changes brought about, changes in law, changes in public attitudes, research into the realities of sexual behavior and education. . . .

We wanted to see those goals achieved by evolutionary methods, not revolutionary methods. We were pretty pure and bland, really. By today's standards we were a bunch of limp-wrist pussyfoots. But we were out of the closet, and that was a very courageous thing in those days because there were not very many of us. . . . We wanted to see changes come about by holding conferences and discussions and becoming subjects for research and telling our story. We wanted to assist people in the academic and behavioral-science world in getting the truth out to people who had an influence on law and law enforcement, the courts, justice, and so on. For example, the Kinsey group in Bloomington, Indiana, was soon in contact with us, and we cooperated with their research.

Today, it may seem needlessly apologetic that the Mattachine Society declared itself "compatible with recognized institutions of a moral and civilized society with respect for the sanctity of the home, church, and state" and encouraged its supporters to dress and behave as model middle-class citizens. "When will the homosexual ever realize that social reform to be effective must be preceded by personal reform?" the *Mattachine Review* pointedly asked in 1956.

Similarly, trusting in scientific neutrality and opening the pages of homophile publications to the viewpoint that homosexuality was a disease requiring prevention and cure today appears naive, timid, or even cowardly. By the standards of today's "queer activism," the fledgling homophile organizations in the years after World War II may have even strengthened the coercive power that psychology and psychiatry wielded over the lives of gay men and lesbians. By leaving social change largely up to the professionals, they appear to have agreed that the experts exerted more control over their lives than many gay men and lesbians did themselves. And perhaps they were right.

During the years when the image of a homosexual menace was so highly charged, pursuing scientific validation was one of the only available strategies for changing public opinion. Moreover, it was an expression of faith in reason during a time of unreason, not to mention the fact that participation in psychological research required real daring for people who had been repeatedly told that they were both sick and immoral. Those involved took real risks. Billie Tallmij (pseudonym), a member of the San Francisco chapter of Daughters of Bilitis during its early years in the mid-1950s, put it this way: "We thought it was very important for women to be studied, so we banged at the door of the Kinsey Institute to try to get some kind of involvement, and we got it. They interviewed us as couples and individuals. Shorty [her lover] and I were both interviewed. Many of the women volunteered. That took real courage."

Homophile activists were not naive about what such research could do. Whether or not to support it, and participate in it, was a matter of constant, heated debate and evaluation. They understood that mental health researchers and professionals could harm as well as help, and they went about recruiting experts with their eyes wide open, for reasons of their own. DOB members Barbara Gittings and Kay Lahusen sarcastically recalled that the meetings of homophile organizations in Philadelphia typically featured

> some psychotherapist or some shrink. Usually some shrink looking for clients to cure. . . . This was an academic exercise. These lectures were really excuses to hold a function to get together and to let people come out a little bit. The content of the lecture didn't really matter that much. It's amazing to people now that we put up with some of the nonsense that was parlayed in these lectures. And yet, we had to go through that because we really needed the recognition that we got from these people who were named in law, the ministry, and the mental health professions. They had credentials and were willing to come to address a meeting of ours instead of just ignoring us entirely. That was important—just their coming and recognizing our existence gave us a boost.

Gittings and Lahusen, who were unusually feisty activists, would sit and listen politely to the experts, then proceed to ignore much of what they said. Professional concern would bring needed attention to the cause of toleration, they trusted. Compared to this important goal, it did not matter all that much that gay men and lesbians believed some of the professionals who promised help and counseled cure were "real stinkers."

Some professionals delivered on their promises, however. In the work of psychologist Evelyn Hooker, the campaign for expert validation and scientific enlightenment paid off. During World War II,

Hooker taught psychology at UCLA and conducted research in the field of animal psychology. Sammy, a young gay man who was a brilliant and enthusiastic student in one of her introductory night courses, befriended Hooker and her husband in 1945. He introduced Hooker to his lover, George, and their circle of friends and then acted as her tour guide through the social networks and institutions of the gay male community in Los Angeles, including drag shows and bars. Hooker reacted with both surprise and pleasure to the "secret world" of Sammy and his peers. Previously, she knew little about homosexuality or homosexuals and was astonished at "the rather extraordinary cross section of society into which I was introduced by Sammy."

"We have let you see us as we are, and now it is your scientific duty to make a study of people like us," Sammy informed his new psychologist friend one night after an evening at the gay club Finocchio's. Hooker later remembered that what he meant was, "We're homosexual, but we don't need psychiatrists. We don't need psychologists. We're not insane. We're not any of those things they say we are."

The result was the very first investigation into whether or not homosexuality was an illness that examined a population of "normal" gay men—men who were not residents of mental hospitals, prisoners, or distressed patients in therapy, but ordinary people living ordinary, if still closeted, lives. For her study, Hooker found subjects mainly through local friendship networks and homophile organizations like the Mattachine Society and ONE, Inc., whose meetings she attended to drum up support. Eventually, she received funding from the National Institute of Mental Health, a federal agency established after World War II to support mental health education, services, and research. Tragically, Sammy was killed in a car accident and did not live to see the impact of the research he had done so much to inspire.

Hooker's study was designed to be straightforward and objective; it was a model of scientific method. It compared a group of 30 gay men with a control group of 30 heterosexual men, all carefully matched for age, education, and I.Q. Hooker gave each of her 60 subjects a battery of psychological and personality tests, including the Rorschach (inkblot) Test, the Thematic Apperception Test (TAT), and the Make a Picture

Story Test. Underlying all of these projective techniques was the theory that subjects would "project" their deepest fears and anxieties into their responses. The tests were supposed to generate a portrait of the basic personality (including sexual orientation) without ever letting subjects know the actual purpose of the research.

Members of the Mattachine Society demonstrate in front of the White House in the early 1960s. The Mattachine Society was one of the pioneering gay civil rights organizations.

When the tests were completed, Hooker handed them over to a panel of three national experts who, without knowing which subjects were homosexual, were asked to rank each one on a scale of psychological adjustment from one (superior) to five (inferior). A majority of all the subjects was assigned the average score of three, proving that the judges had been completely unable to identify the homosexual subjects in the study. "Homosexuality as a clinical entity does not exist," Hooker reasoned on the basis of her data. "Homosexuality may be a deviation in sexual pattern which is within the normal range psychologically." In other words, no necessary correlation existed between homosexuality and psychological impairment or abnormality.

It is much easier to understand Hooker's point in retrospect because her view is more widespread today. Being stigmatized and burdened with secrecy *does* produce numerous problems, of course, and gay individuals are still disproportionately victimized by alcoholism, teen suicide, and other tragedies that twist the emotions and distort the personality. But we understand these tragedies to be the consequences of social oppression rather than logical outgrowths of homosexuality itself. Considered separately from the disastrous impact of homophobia, homosexuality is psychologically neutral: it may not guarantee emotional health, but it certainly does not produce emotional sickness. This is what Hooker showed, and these results were shocking at the time. If there was one thing most psychological experts agreed about in the 1950s, it was that homosexuals were not normal; in fact, they were sick. Somehow (though plenty of disagreement existed about exactly how) they were different and identifiable precisely because they were different. "Every clinical psychologist worth his soul would tell you that if he gave those projective tests he could tell whether a person was gay or not," Hooker remembered. "I showed that they couldn't do it." Her work not only undermined the conventional view that homosexuality was a form of mental disturbance but showed that orthodox psychiatric approaches—theoretical and clinical—were distorted and wrong.

In 1956, Hooker presented her findings—that no psychological differences existed between homosexual and heterosexual men—before the annual meetings of the American Psychological Association. Hundreds of people attended her lecture, "The Adjustment of the Male Overt Homosexual." The atmosphere was tense and sometimes angry; the psychoanalysts "would as soon shoot me as look at me," she said at the time. Still, the exceptional character of her work was clear and, in later years, she was awarded numerous professional honors for her pioneering research on "normal" homosexuals. In September 1967, for example, she was appointed chair of the National Institute of Mental Health Task Force on Homosexuality. Because of Hooker's presence, the conclusions of this government investigation were remarkably progressive. Along with the standard references to "prevention" and "cure," recommendations made by the task force included changing social policy to reduce the "injustice and suffering" experienced by homosexuals.

Unlike Kinsey, who always maintained that devotion to science prevented him from active involvement in political or social causes, Evelyn Hooker intentionally combined advocacy with objective re-search throughout her career because she believed that freedom from stigma and rejection would eliminate whatever "abnormal" behavioral patterns homosexuals did exhibit. Her activist stance was quite daring for a scientist, but there were limits to what Hooker could do or say. She attended DOB meetings, for example, but readily admitted that she could never have conducted successful research on lesbians; the pre-dictable suspicions about her own sexuality would have brought her professional career to a premature end. "Dr. Hooker wouldn't touch the Daughters with a ten-foot-pole—no one had touched women," one San Francisco lesbian remembered. "Nonetheless, Dr. Hooker was a very close friend."

As a "very close friend," Hooker wrote and spoke out on behalf of homosexuals and homophile organizations, whose members had not only helped to supply her with research subjects but had followed her progress with tremendous care and interest. "Inverts Are Not a Distinct Personality Type," announced the first issue of the *Mattachine Review,* the first openly homosexual publication in the United States, dedicated to the liberal view that homosexuals were just like everyone else and not frighteningly different in behavior and attitude. The *Mattachine*

Review not only summarized Hooker's work but reported on other ongoing psychological studies. "Science Wins Out," the editors of the *Review* proclaimed excitedly when Hooker spoke before her American Psychiatric Association (APA) colleagues in 1956: "The implications of her work are almost limitless, as can readily be seen. There is little doubt that psychology, psychiatry, medicine and the law will be compelled to revise much of their thinking and radically alter many attitudes and practices as her work becomes more widely known."

7

Of Causes and Cures

TOPPLING THE OLD IDEAS and prejudices about homosexuality was not easy, and it did not happen quickly. During the 1950s and early 1960s, the weight of psychological authority was not with Hooker but against her. In fact, during these years, the notion that homosexuality was a mental illness spread far and wide. It was not uncommon for same-sex intimacy to be discussed alongside schizophrenia, paranoia, manic depression, alcoholism, and other types of emotional instability that often led to suicide. Some experts considered homosexuality to be the cause of major personality disorders; others considered homosexuality a symptom. Virtually all of them considered it a sickness.

One of the few studies devoted to lesbianism in the late 1950s, *Voyage from Lesbos,* concluded that "homosexuality is the symptom of an illness. . . . Most homosexuals are unhappy, suffering people." Psychoanalyst Edmund Bergler insisted time and time again

One of the most persistent myths about male homosexuality is that it is caused by an overly close relationship between a young boy and his mother. In fact, researchers remain uncertain about what causes sexual orientation.

during the 1950s and 1960s that "*there are no healthy homosexuals.*" He wrote that "homosexual society, in which membership is attained through individual psychopathology, is neither 'healthy' nor happy. Life within this society tends to reinforce, fixate, and add new disturbing elements to the entrenched psychopathology of its members." Experts and ordinary citizens alike paid close attention to the views of Bergler, who was among a handful of nationally recognized authorities on homosexuality. The author of such books as *Homosexuality: Disease or Way of Life?*, Bergler often spoke about the topic on radio and wrote numerous articles in popular magazines such as *Cosmopolitan* as well as in professional journals.

Clinicians such as Bergler always swore that their intentions were good and that their attitudes were well ahead of other Americans. They were, after all, members of the "helping professions," sworn to uphold and promote the welfare of their patients. "The therapeutic pessimism of the past is gradually disappearing," Bergler noted with great relief. "*Today, psychiatric-psychoanalytic treatment can cure homosexuality,*" so long as that treatment is "of one to two years' duration, with a minimum of three appointments each week—*provided the patient really wishes to change. . . . The homosexual's real enemy is not his perversion, but his ignorance of the possibility that he can be helped.*" Many others shared this smug attitude of professional benevolence, confident that pathologizing homosexuality was a tremendous advance over punishing it with criminal penalties. In 1955, the liberal Group for the Advancement of Psychiatry reported: "Like the individual with a physical illness, the homosexual should be encouraged to seek treatment, and a therapeutic attitude should be maintained even when such individuals are segregated by society. Psychotherapy, particularly psychoanalysis, offers the greatest probability of benefit."

The difference between enlightened scientific opinion and simple prejudice was frequently hard to distinguish, however. In 1956, the same year Hooker publicly presented her groundbreaking research, Bergler wrote that the homosexual character contained

a mixture of superciliousness, fake aggression, and whimpering. Like all psychic masochists, they are subservient when confronted with a stronger person, merciless when in power, unscrupulous about trampling on a weaker person. The only language their unconscious understands is brute force. What is most discouraging, you seldom find an intact ego (what is popularly called a "correct person") among them.

Not only did homosexuals suffer from mental illness, according to Bergler, but they also had a perverse need to inflict suffering on others because they were filled with savage hatred. They could be so destructive that a wide range of severe antihomosexual laws were necessary, especially for the protection of minors. Today, these ideas appear obsolete, and Bergler's tone seems shocking, insensitive, and crude. But at the time, most people, and definitely most experts, agreed with his sentiments. They rejected the notion of a happy or healthy homosexual and held fast to a view of homosexuality as an illness in desperate need of cure.

The widespread belief that homosexuality and homosexuals were abnormal resulted partly from specific explanations of what caused men and women to be gay. Bergler, for example, argued that homosexuality (in both men and women) was an inferior solution to the conflict every growing child faced in controlling unconscious aggression against the mother. But the equation between homosexuality and mental illness also grew out of general trends that made more people psychologically abnormal than ever before. The two decades after World War II were the golden age of psychoanalysis in the United States. The war appeared to have validated psychodynamic approaches, and, along with an influx of European psychoanalysts fleeing Hitler, simplified Freudian themes spread rapidly throughout popular culture. Although the number of formally trained analysts (and their patients) were never very large, psychoanalytic approaches to mental illness and its treatment had a huge impact on professionals outside of psychoanalysis and on public consciousness in general.

Hollywood, for example, produced a gush of movies about mental disturbance and the shocking conditions of mental institutions that turned psychotherapists into familiar figures, at least on the silver screen. In 1942, Bette Davis played the part of a troubled woman who was transformed through psychiatric treatment in *Now, Voyager.* Other popular films concerned with emotional healing included Alfred Hitch-cock's *Spellbound,* starring Ingrid Bergman and Gregory Peck (1945), *The Three Faces of Eve,* featuring Joanne Woodward (1957), and *Three on a Couch* (1966), with Jerry Lewis and Janet Leigh. Although the way psychiatric experts were portrayed in these films varied—sometimes they were kind and benevolent, sometimes silly or even sinister—the viewing public rapidly absorbed a vocabulary filled with complexes, dream interpretation, and repression.

By exposing Americans to maladjusted personalities and deviant (but fascinating) behaviors, movies frequently reinforced Joseph McCarthy's point that difference was dangerous and something to be avoided at all costs. Differences in sexual orientation, however, were treated only indirectly during the 1940s and 1950s. Heterosexual characters, if they tended toward sissiness or being butch, were viewed with suspicion. Explicitly gay and lesbian characters, on the other hand, were thoroughly invisible during this bland time. The motion picture production code, by which Hollywood voluntarily regulated itself, prohibited the portrayal of homosexuality until 1961. Even the words "homosexual" and "homosexuality" were banned. During the 1960s, when homo-sexuals began to appear on screen occasionally—as in *The Children's Hour, The Killing of Sister George,* and *The Boys in the Band*—they were typically sadistic and pathetic figures, filled with self-loathing and aware that they were afflicted by a horrible mental condition. During the 1950s and 1960s, the movies Americans watched certainly reflected the mood of conformity, but Hollywood also satisfied the public's curiosity about mental disturbance, increased public awareness of psychological abnormality, and helped to create a market for the experts who claimed they could understand and fix the suffering human psyche.

Popular magazines also ran numerous features about the talents of mental healing and healers. "Are you always worrying?" a *Time* maga-zine headline inquired in 1948, above a flattering portrait of William "Dr. Will" Menninger, member of the country's first family of psychia-try, the Menningers of Topeka, Kansas. "Does your family have a neurosis?" asked *Collier's* magazine a few years later. "This is the age of psychology and psychoanalysis as much as it is the age of chemistry or

In the 1950s, the Menningers—father C. F. (center) and sons Karl (left) and Will (right)—were regarded as the nation's first family of psychiatry. The Menningers were instrumental in bringing about a surge of popular interest in psychiatry and psychology in the early 1950s.

the atom bomb," announced *Life* in 1957 in the debut of an admiring five-part series on the "brand-new and strictly American" science of the mind. Author Ernest Havemann estimated that 9 out of 10 daily newspapers carried at least one psychological advice column, reported on such surprising best-sellers as *The Basic Writings of Sigmund Freud,* and pointed out that more psychologists and psychiatrists were at work in the United States than in any other country on earth.

Although years earlier the Kinsey reports had effectively communicated that homosexuality was quite common, magazines began paying close attention to homosexuality only in the early 1960s, at which time it was consistently presented as a tragic and possibly contagious condition for which science might find a cure. "A secret world grows open and bolder," *Life* proclaimed in dismay in June 1964.

> Society is forced to look at it—and try to understand it. . . . This social disorder, which society tries to suppress, has forced itself into the public eye because it does present a problem—and parents especially are concerned.

The desire to reach a mass audience was evident among psychological experts, who actively marketed their services after the war and insisted that emotional problems could be solved with the right professional help. According to William Menninger, "no misconception in psychiatry is more widespread than the fact that most individuals who have had a mental illness cannot get well, or that those who do remain something of a liability to themselves or their families or communities. The great, great majority of psychiatric patients recover!" On top of this extreme optimism, which was so characteristic of the postwar years, the definition of psychological abnormality began to stretch, so that virtually everyone came under the watchful eyes of therapeutic helpers. In theory at least, psychotherapy could benefit even the most well-adjusted people. Since healthy individuals could abruptly lose their mental balance and descend into anxiety and hopelessness, psychotherapy evolved into "the process by which *normality is created.*" "Normal neurosis," it seemed, was everywhere.

In a booming postwar economy that prided itself on meeting the expanding needs of each and every American, peace of mind, like cars and houses, was for sale to interested consumers. "Good mental health or well-being is a commodity which can be created under favorable circumstances," psychiatrist Henry Brosin predicted at the end of World War II. The sales pitch for mental health was so effective and the public demand for counseling services so intense that experts soon found themselves in the odd position of needing to dampen the public's enthusiasm. Karen Horney, a dedicated and influential follower of Freud, went so far as to write *Are You Considering Psychoanalysis?* in order "to dispel mysterious notions about analysis by removing unrealistic expectations of a magic cure." But magic cures and faith in analysis were the order of the day, and nowhere was this clearer than in emphatic efforts to pathologize and change homosexuality.

The very first edition of psychiatry's diagnostic bible, called the *Diagnostic and Statistical Manual: Mental Disorders,* or *(DSM),* was published in 1952. Although the first Kinsey report had documented the wide variety of sexual behaviors and orientations among men several years earlier, the *DSM* listed homosexuality as a "sociopathic personality disturbance"—alongside addiction and antisocial reaction—and it

Though she founded the American Institute of Psychoanalysis, the eminent psychiatrist Karen Horney nevertheless cautioned against an unrealistic overreliance on psychoanalysis as a "magic cure" for every manner of personal problem.

remained there, unchallenged, until 1968. The "sexual deviation" classification (which was a subset of the larger category "personality disorders") included "homosexuality, transvestism, pedophilia, fetishism, and sexual sadism (including rape, sexual assault, mutilation)."

Although personality disorders were considered extremely serious mental illnesses—some of the others were schizoid, paranoid, emotionally unstable, passive-aggressive, and compulsive personalities—cure was possible. Because these disorders were considered to be purely psychological in origin and not the outcome of physiological problems such as brain damage, they could be treated and eliminated, at least in theory. With the correct psychotherapy and proper motivation on the part of the affected individual, homosexual illness could be replaced by heterosexual health.

During the early years of the cold war, the most influential theories about the origin and treatment of male homosexuality were Freudian, which is not that surprising considering the cultural popularity of Freudian psychology and the tendency (already evident during World War II) to blame mothers for everything from trivial personal problems to national and international disasters. The most vocal psychoanalysts after World War II, however, rejected Freud's view that bisexuality was an innate element of human sexuality. Because they insisted that heterosexuality was the only normal psychological drive and maintained that it was "biologically programmed," they were also much more optimistic than Freud had been about the possibilities of altering homosexual orientation.

Although members of the psychoanalytic community loved to squabble over the details, they did agree that homosexuality could be traced to failures in early childhood development and fears of the opposite sex, a view that was successfully communicated to the general public, including gay men and lesbians themselves. One gay man wrote anonymously to psychiatrist Edward Strecker in 1946:

Dear Professor Strecker,

I am a sixteen-year-old boy; a "sissy," a "mother's boy." I am ashamed to take my problem to my parents or to a doctor whom I would have to see, so I am writing to you. Please try to understand and help me. I guess I am a homosexual. (It hurts me deeply to say, think, or write that word. Even to hear it!) . . . My mother is what I suppose you would call "frigid." She said she dreaded the thought of sexual relations and was engaged seven times before she married Daddy (she was very beautiful and popular, though). Could this have anything to do with my troubles?

"Absolutely," replied Strecker. "Mom . . . has poisoned the boy's mind against normal, mature heterosexual living."

Clearly the analytic view was more than an abstract theory popular among experts. It was a powerful force in gay and lesbian lives, deeply affecting the way men and women understood their past emotional development and possibilities of future happiness. Even contributors to homophile publications sometimes expressed the belief that they were less than whole human beings and showed that they were well versed in the concepts and language of psychology. "Many of us homosexuals regard our inversion as a handicap because it precludes a complete life," wrote Carl Hardin in a 1956 letter to the *Mattachine Review*. "And no life is complete emotionally or biologically without the extension of love in the upbringing of children of one's own. And this limitation on our lives imposed upon us in our childhood could have been prevented in most cases. . . . To boast of being glad for an exclusively homosexual condition is but a defense mechanism."

As time passed, the analytic view wore thin. But for some gay men and lesbians, especially those who came of age in the years right after World War II, it never disappeared. In 1962, gay writer Donald Webster Cory argued that acceptance and integration were impossible goals "so long as [gay men and lesbians] state that the dirtiest word in the English language is a four-letter monosyllable—cure." Thirteen years later, in 1975, Cory was still writing that "the struggle for justice should not be turned into a struggle for encouragement of homosexual development."

During the golden age of psychoanalysis, Irving Bieber's work on male homosexuality was *the* standard reference. Anyone who had anything to say about homosexuality in the late 1950s and 1960s quoted his study of male homosexuals, which consolidated 106 case studies contributed by 77 psychiatrists (all members of the Society of Medical

Though psychoanalysis was once regarded as an exotic and somewhat dubious foreign science, by the end of the 1950s images such as this one, of an analysand and his physician, permeated popular culture.

Psychoanalysis) during the 1950s. It was by far the largest sample that had ever been used in psychoanalytic research on homosexuality, but like earlier studies, all of the subjects were undergoing treatment, and a majority of them (64 percent) wished they were not homosexual. Bieber and his collaborators did not seek to include the ordinary, "normal" homosexuals who had intrigued Evelyn Hooker.

Not surprisingly, Bieber's *Homosexuality: A Psychoanalytic Study of Male Homosexuals* did not bother to ask whether same-sex intimacy was normal or abnormal, healthy or pathological. "All psychoanalytic theories assume adult homosexuality is psychopathologic," Bieber asserted without comment at the outset. His two main goals were to explain homosexuality's psychological origins and outline a method of cure.

The causes were to be found in childhood and the family. Parents, "the architects of family structure," were at fault. "Personality maladaptation is the objective manifestation of dysfunction in the family," Bieber suggested in a wordy formulation, "and the development of personality disorders in a child is almost always evidence of the pervasive effects of parental psychopathology." Families that included overbearing mothers—Bieber's term for them was "close-binding intimate," or CBI—were the most likely to produce male homosexuals. Seventy-three percent of the homosexuals in Bieber's sample had such mothers, in comparison to only 32 percent of the heterosexual control group.

These women were obviously the culprits. They were, according to Bieber, controlling, possessive, seductive, and overly intimate with their sons, whom they preferred to their husbands and other children. According to Bieber, CBI mothers interfered with their sons' natural heterosexual inclinations, blocked the necessary identification between sons and their fathers, and prohibited rough-and-tumble boyhood friendships that could foster appropriate masculinity. By babying and overprotecting their sons, these disturbed women caused them to become homosexual. Bieber pointed out that homosexuals also had defective relationships with their fathers. Distance and hostility between fathers and sons were almost as common as intimacy with an overbearing mother, and 30 percent of the research subjects were unlucky enough to have both. But fathers, if they were normal, could also come to their sons' rescue, neutralizing "deleterious maternal influences" and "mother fixation" and preventing homosexuality from taking root. In the end, it was neurotic mothers, many "burdened by deep-going homosexual problems" of their own, who were to blame.

The general picture that emerged from Bieber's study was of a sick family, a "triangular system" in which sons became homosexual

73

through no fault of their own. Sexually overstimulated and restricted at the same time by their mothers, "prehomosexual" boys also lived in constant fear of being physically and emotionally harmed by their fathers. "*The H-son* [homosexual son] *emerged as the interactional focal point upon whom the most profound parental psychopathology was concentrated.*" Innocent victims of extremely disturbed parents, who were incapable of healthy relationships themselves, these sons developed abnormal fears of women and of heterosexuality. They worried about injury to their penises and felt terror at the thought or sight of female genitals. Excessively dependent upon their mothers and rejected by their peers, these sons were already marked by self-contempt and impotence by the time they reached adolescence. In desperation, these unfortunates turned to boys and men for sexual satisfaction.

Because heterosexuality was "the biologic norm," however, there was hope for change. Normal impulses always lurked within homosexuals, and these impulses could be encouraged with the proper techniques. Unlike Freud, who had criticized "therapeutic enthusiasts" as unrealistic, Bieber and the post–World War II analytic generation committed themselves to the project of actively changing sexual orientation. To help patients "adjust" to their homosexuality, they explained, was to do them a terrible disservice. Traces of heterosexual desire were almost always present, Bieber argued, and the prognosis for cure was especially hopeful with patients who were young and willing to undergo long-term psychoanalysis. His study reported that

> *29 patients had become exclusively heterosexual during the course of psychoanalytic treatment.* . . . the most optimistic and promising results thus far reported. . . . Although this change may be more easily accomplished by some than by others, in our judgment a heterosexual shift is a possibility for all homosexuals who are strongly motivated to change.

But even his own numbers showed that Bieber was stretching the truth in his zeal to make the case for cure. Of the 72 men who were exclusively homosexual at the beginning of analysis, only 14 had become exclusively heterosexual and another 14 had become bisexual. (Bieber did not specify whether conversion to "exclusive" heterosexuality implied a change in behavior alone or whether it also required a wholesale alteration in a man's erotic fantasies and emotional orientation.) Forty-two of these men, or 57 percent, had not changed at all.

Pathological parents were also responsible for causing homosexuality in their daughters, although studies of lesbians were much rarer than studies of gay men. Proponents of psychoanalysis believed that a defective upbringing would turn innocent young girls into self-loathing and suicide-prone adult lesbians who were terrified of heterosexual intercourse and hostile toward men in general. Charles Socarides, an analyst who during the 1950s and 1960s was, along with Irving Bieber, largely responsible for advancing the idea that homosexuality was a curable mental illness, claimed that the lesbian experienced "murderous fantasies toward her mother" that could be traced back to early infancy. Psychosexual development had taken a wrong turn with these female babies, and as a result they were destined to spend their adult lives desperately acting out disturbed needs for maternal attention and trying to recapture a state of infantile dependency. He explained:

> These unconscious impulses [toward the mother] are resisted and, as a reaction to them, unconscious guilt toward the mother is generated. Hate impulses are then transformed into a masochistic libidinal attitude which disguises her hateful feelings, diminishes her guilt and punishes her through suffering.

Many homophile advocates adopted these ideas as well, though their loyalties were to lesbians themselves rather than to Freud and his legacy. Donald Webster Cory conducted 100 interviews with lesbians, many of them members of DOB, for his 1964 book *The Lesbian in America*. Cory remarked,

> Most lesbians, but not all, reflect the newer scientific thinking, and readily admit that they must have had childhood problems that led them to their present course of life. A few, particularly if they are professionally trained in psychology, or have undergone therapy (especially by orthodox Freudians) are rather sophisticated on this subject. They will tell of difficulties between their parents, lack of a good mother image, overinvolvement with a father. . . .

Many of the women he interviewed reported strong bonds with their fathers and brothers and poor relations with their mothers, childhood sexual traumas that may have frightened them away from men, and an abundance of tomboyish behavior. They were not only familiar with the psychoanalytic view of homosexuality but, for better or worse, they used it as a way of understanding themselves and their lives.

There was more optimism about treating and preventing homosexuality in the decades after World War II than at any other time during the 20th century, and psychoanalysis promised the most culturally visible "cure" during these years. Analysis was not the only available technique for the reform of homosexual orientation, however. Ever since the late 19th century, medical and psychological professionals had suggested strategies ranging from total rest and hypnosis to cold baths and vigorous physical exercise. In 1892, Dr. Graeme M. Hammond announced that "I have found nothing more serviceable than the bicycle to accomplish this object." Throughout the century, experts periodically insisted that the road to heterosexuality was paved with practice, pure and simple. "There is only one way that the homosexual can overcome his phobia and learn to have heterosexual intercourse," Lionel Ovesey stated flatly in 1965, "and that way is in bed with a woman." Marriage to an extremely patient woman was counseled as something worth trying. So were "educational" visits to prostitutes, at least for men.

More behaviorally and biologically inclined experts offered a menu of options as well. They experimented with aversive treatments, surgery, drugs, and even acupuncture—all of which had the advantage of being much faster and usually less costly than years on an analyst's couch. Aversive therapies depended largely upon methods of behavior modification through negative reinforcement. They were designed to drive people away from homosexuality by associating it with punitive and repulsive experiences. "Faradic therapy," as electric shock used to be called, involved showing images of male nudes to gay men, and then shocking them with low levels of electricity if they became sexually aroused. Methods of "covert desensitization" were also tried, based on purely imaginary disgust rather than physiological stimuli. Clinical use of aversive therapies continued well into the 1970s. One 1972 study, for example, reported on 40 subjects who had endured five days of shock treatments, for a total of 1,050 shocks each. Even at this late date, the authors made no comment about the ethical dilemmas of this type of "help."

Behavioral reinforcement could be positive as well as negative. The same men who were "punished" for their attraction to other men might

The Rorschach Test was a frequently used tool of the psychiatric profession in the 1950s. The response of a patient when asked to provide verbal or written interpretations of inkblot designs such as this one was understood to provide indicators of his or her mental or emotional state.

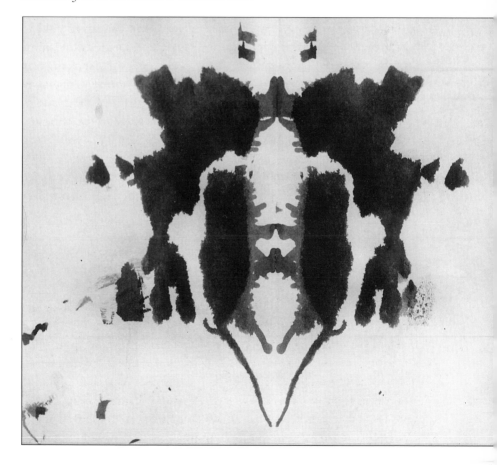

be "rewarded" (no shocks were administered) if they responded positively to images of scantily clad or naked women. In the early 1960s, two enterprising researchers in the field of aversive therapy went so far as to offer detailed instructions for constructing a simple shocking device that could be used in the privacy of one's own home! Aversive behavioral therapy sometimes involved chemicals rather than electric shocks. The chemicals induced convulsions or severe nausea, but the underlying principles of this "treatment" were the same.

Surgical approaches concentrated on the genitals and brains of homosexual subjects, many of whom were prisoners or mental patients. Male and female castration was sometimes performed on the theory that homosexuals were oversexed. Experimental procedures such as testicle transplantation and clitoral alterations (intended to decrease the alleged hypersensitivity of lesbians' genitals) are also documented in the medical literature. Lobotomies were a popular choice as well, especially in psychosurgery's heyday right after World War II. But brain surgery for the purpose of eradicating homosexuality was performed by some physicians up through the 1970s, and the notion that homosexual attraction is rooted in the brain—rather than in other parts of the human body or in the psyche—remains popular today.

Finally, there have been drugs, which are sometimes combined with other methods of cure, such as psychotherapy. Cocaine solutions and strychnine injections were tried early in the century by one doctor, Denslow Lewis, who was determined to eliminate lesbians' "pernicious practices." When hormones were first isolated and mass-produced in the late 1920s and 1930s, some experimenters suspected that homosexuality was due to an imbalance of male and female chemistry within the body, and they began treating homosexuals with both androgens (male hormones) and estrogens (female hormones). In recent decades, hormonal drug therapy has become more common in prison populations, and judges have sometimes stipulated drug treatment in sentences for criminal sex offenders.

All of these cures—psychoanalytic, behavioral, surgical, and chemical—assumed that homosexuality was an illness that should be eradicated if at all possible. Although they were united in insisting that the treatment was for their patients' own good, the experts rarely agreed about the effectiveness of their techniques. What actually were the "success rates" of psychoanalysis or aversion therapy in converting homosexuals to heterosexuality?

Psychoanalysts tended to make exaggerated claims that their cure was the best and only cure, as we have already seen in the case of Irving Bieber. Because of the popularity of Freudian psychology after 1945, psychoanalysts frequently dismissed evidence that sexual orientation was extremely difficult to change. Sometimes they ignored it entirely. But advocates of behavioral cures were equally proud of their successes and promised that as many as half of all their patients could expect a significant reduction in homosexual feelings and behaviors. In 1976, three years *after* the American Psychiatric Association had decided that homosexuality no longer qualified as a mental illness, a comprehensive review of all types of treatments aimed at curing homosexuality documented success rates ranging from 27 to 47 percent. The author of the report, Jerome D. Frank, a Johns Hopkins psychiatrist and expert on psychotherapy, criticized research in the field for its shoddy design and use of easily distorted data. But he still concluded that

> between 10 percent and 20 percent of those with an exclusively homosexual adjustment can be helped to shift significantly toward a heterosexual one, and of bisexuals up to 40 percent could become essentially heterosexual. . . . It would be desirable . . . to combat the sense of hopelessness and inevitability so prevalent among homosexuals by widely publicizing the fact that current treatment methods enable about one-fifth of exclusive homosexuals to achieve some heterosexual interests and competence if they really wish to do so.

8

Experts on Our Own Lives

Frank Kameny, one of the early presidents of the Washington, D.C., Mattachine Society, was one of the first gay rights activists to attack the authority of the psychiatric establishment, which then officially regarded homosexuality as an illness.

BY THE EARLY 1960s, activists had begun to grow tired of all the talk about cures. They could no longer contain their anger at the self-righteousness of experts like Bergler, Bieber, and Socarides. The tone of discussion among gay men and lesbians began to change decisively, moving from deep respect for psychological experts to suspicion of them and their motives. Bergler was skewered as a pompous windbag who had abandoned science for a "maniacal moralism." The names of Irving Bieber and Charles Socarides became code words for all the worst that psychiatry had ever had to say about homosexuality.

But the psychological status of homosexuality still remained central. "I feel that the entire homophile movement . . . is going to stand or fall upon the question of whether or not homosexuality is a sickness," declared Frank Kameny, president of the Washington, D.C., chapter of the Mattachine Society.

Kameny had served in World War II and then been fired from his civil service job as an army astronomer in 1957 for being gay. Unhappy with the "bland, unassertive, and apologetic" tone of homophile activism, Kameny mounted a forceful and articulate critique of psychiatric authority. "I for one am not prepared to play a passive role in . . . controversies over psychopathology letting others dispose of me as they see fit. I intend to play an active role in the determination of my fate." Following Kameny's bold lead, Mattachine members in Washington, D.C., and elsewhere finally adopted a resolution in 1965 stating that homosexuality was not a "sickness" but "merely a preference, orientation, or propensity, on a par with, and not different in kind from, heterosexuality." The antisickness statement was controversial among homophile activists, but their reluctance to challenge the psychological establishment so directly was beginning to give way to a new mood of self-reliance. As Barbara Gittings, whose psychiatrist had promised to cure her during her first year in college, recalled,

> We were mired in the psychiatric outlook on homosexuality which was very difficult to move away from. Frank's statement was a major breakthrough for us. It was adopted eventually by virtually all of the gay organizations then in existence on the East coast and gradually by others around the country. The statement was important because it finally said, "Look, they are the ones who are creating the problem, we're going to step away from it. Our problem is one of civil rights and we're going to go out and get our civil rights. The psychiatrists can go wallow in their own stuff."

Once homosexuals began thinking of themselves as experts, the tactics and aims of homophile activism changed radically. Inspired by the model of the civil rights movement, which demonstrated the moral force of African Americans taking their destinies into their own hands, gay men and lesbians moved away from the hope that scientific experts could promote understanding. Instead, they seized upon direct collective action as the best way to defend *homosexuality* itself, not just individual men and women who were unlucky enough to be homosexual. One lesbian put it this way in the early 1960s: "If people think of us as different, and not sick, we'd be okay. We have to change the world—not us. A society that hates and discriminates is sick—not me." Public understanding was still an important goal, but self-acceptance and social change took priority on the activist agenda.

In this new light, every word that psychological experts had written about homosexuality, and every treatment they had offered, looked much different than it had just a few years earlier. Psychotherapists after Stonewall began to look as much like sinister enemies as compassionate healers. No longer did activists debate the technical details of conversion to heterosexuality or argue about the merits of one brand of cure or another. Techniques designed to alter sexual orientation became morally suspect in and of themselves.

Tales of failed "cures" began to circulate. After 1969, testimonials from gay men and lesbians who revealed how they had been treated at the hands of "helping professionals" provided the gay movement with some of its most persuasive evidence for the depth of homophobia and the need for social change. Personal stories were extremely compelling not only because they were personal, but because they showed how easily experts could humiliate the tormented homosexuals who sought their aid while still commanding unbelievable loyalty and trust. Psychotherapy was not simply an insult. It was an insult in which many gay men and lesbians had once placed their faith.

In 1971, for example, Christopher Z. Hobson described how he had "survived" fourteen years of psychotherapy, finally coming to terms with his sexuality thanks only to the gay movement. Beginning in his last year of high school, Hobson sought out a series of therapists, "basically because I desperately wanted to be heterosexual." He stayed in therapy for years, "eager for punishment, and eager for acceptance." But he found no answers to his most agonizing questions and no relief from his own guilt. Only after some of his friends got involved in the women's movement did he realize that "the therapists *failed to help me understand my situation*—to overcome my own lack of understanding." Suddenly, it was clear that his therapists' failure "resulted from their assumption that I was, by definition, sick—that homosexuality (but not heterosexuality) is a pathology." Hobson finally quit psychotherapy in disgust after his therapist told him that there were no gay psychoanalysts

(Hobson knew otherwise) and found the courage to come out in the gay movement. "All over the United States," he wrote, "there are thousands in psychotherapy, and millions more under the pervasive social influence of psychiatric dogma, who will never make this step [coming out] until they are reached not by doctors, but by the winds of social protest."

Some of the most poignant stories about the quest for a cure came from established older men who had literally spent all of their adult lives seeking to eradicate a profound aspect of their identities. Dr. Howard Brown, former New York City health services administrator and chair of the National Gay Task Force, spoke publicly to his medical colleagues in October 1973 about his anguish at having resigned his post because of a reporter's threat to expose all the homosexuals in Mayor John Lindsay's administration: "I saw myself accused of being myself, and I felt utterly defenseless." Even after his coming-out speech was noted on the front page of the *New York Times,* Brown felt very different from the young gay and lesbian activists he saw around him, who "rejected the respectability I had worked so hard to achieve. . . . I still accepted many of the psychiatric clichés about homosexuals—that we were emotionally impaired narcissists who could never love as fully as heterosexuals, that we were innately superficial and irresponsible."

Brown's own personal encounter with psychiatry had begun in 1942 as he was planning to enter medical school. He anxiously revealed his secret to a psychiatrist, who responded by assuring Brown that he must be mistaken because "homosexuals don't become doctors, they become hairdressers." During his military service, Brown studied the army's diagnostic listings only to discover that homosexuals, such as himself, were being classified as "constitutional psychopathic inferiors." In medical school, his textbooks taught him that homosexual patients were impulsive, immature, and had little if any "consideration for the ordinary moral concepts and standards of the group in which they live." Plagued by a feeling of impending doom and certain that he would lead a miserable life, Brown entered psychoanalysis. Four times each week for four long years, he talked about his dreams and wound up spending more money than on all of his other living expenses combined. "Dr.

Snell [a pseudonym] convinced me that I could not love—indeed, that no homosexual could love. . . . It took me almost twenty years to recover from the effects of my analysis—which is to say, it took me almost twenty years to regard myself and other homosexuals as worthwhile and capable." On the basis of his own experience, Brown concluded that "it would have been better for us if psychiatrists had ignored homosexuality altogether, but they have not. Instead, they have actively used their position of power and respect to make our lives more difficult."

Martin Duberman, an award-winning historian and playwright, also described in very personal terms how the desperate quest for a cure could contaminate and control a life otherwise characterized by tremendous achievement. As he moved from one elite institution to another—first Harvard, then Yale and Princeton—Duberman lived a life split violently in two: a charmed academic career alongside a hellish inner life. In his 1991 memoir, *Cures,* he recalled,

> The more secure I became in my status as an intellectual, the less gloom I felt about being—as the psychiatric establishment then insisted—a disabled human being. I did implicitly accept the culture's verdict that I was defective, but could now somewhat circumscribe the indictment; I no longer felt *wholly* unworthy—merely crippled in my affective life.

In 1957, when Duberman began his lengthy career in psychotherapy, he had not heard of Evelyn Hooker, nor was he aware of fledgling homophile organizations like the Mattachine Society. He certainly did not take seriously the possibility that his own homosexual feelings might be "normal." Instead, he wrote to Edmund Bergler pleading for help and began working with a series of therapists in an effort to change himself.

His civil rights activism during the 1960s and his numerous literary efforts on behalf of the anti–Vietnam War movement distracted him from the "formal, obsessive analysis of who I was" and helped him feel better about himself. But unlike Christopher Hobson, Duberman did not gain a sense of personal release from political involvement, none of which was in gay organizations. It would be years before he considered the idea that his identity as a gay man might have more to do with cultural oppression than with emotional disorder. The damaging lessons repeated like mantras in his therapy sessions—that he was sick, immature, and incomplete—remained fixed in his mind until after Stonewall. Following New York's first Gay Pride march in 1970, Duberman wrote in his diary that the participants were nothing but "cripples on yet another march to a faith healing shrine."

Duberman's therapist during the 1960s, Karl (a pseudonym), subscribed to the popular outlines of the analytic fix. Karl told Duberman that his relationship with his mother was at fault and that abandoning that "unhealthily symbiotic" relationship was a first step toward becoming heterosexual. He assured Duberman that, with some effort, his "heterosexual leanings could be unblocked." And he counseled that developing a "trusting relationship with an older man"—by which Karl meant himself—was necessary "if you are ever to heal the scars of having grown up with a detached father."

After Stonewall, and after his fortieth birthday in 1970, Duberman inched his way into the gay movement. He gathered up his courage and quit therapy with Karl, came out in a *New York Times* article in 1971 and then a book he published in 1972, got involved with the Gay Academic Union, and found the courage to debate Irving Bieber in a public forum at Columbia University. "I didn't feel that I deserved the comfort," he remembered thinking in 1970. "I was in no shape simply to embrace freedom; I trailed so many negative attitudes about myself that the process of peeling them away still continues to the present day."

Although the total number of gay men who had been through classical psychoanalysis was always small—it was far too expensive for most people to afford—even fewer lesbians published first-person accounts of their experiences in therapy during the 1950s and 1960s. Still, there is reason to believe that interactions between lesbians and mental health professionals were quite similar to those described by their male counterparts. "It didn't work," Joy Tomchin commented flatly on her stint in psychoanalysis during the mid-1960s. "But I had a goal of becoming straight. I didn't see any life for myself as a gay person at that time."

No matter what patients were doing or feeling when they entered therapy, clinicians automatically assumed that their sexual orientation was the problem to be solved. Lesbians were repeatedly told that their feelings of emotional and sexual connection with other women were abnormal and tragic and that they were fixated on their mothers, who had caused them to develop in a deviant direction from a young age. "You're very lucky that you haven't committed suicide because you're a lesbian," one woman recalled her female analyst saying. "There might be hope for you." Another woman, who sought psychiatric help for problem drinking when her lover of many years did indeed commit suicide, was hospitalized for 15 months, kept in "preventive" seclusion, and heavily tranquilized. Doctors informed her that she "was utterly dependent (love women); had anxiety neuroses (alcohol withdrawal); was borderline schizophrenic (failed to conform to their idea of what a woman's life should be); and had a poor prognosis (I believed in myself more than in their theories about me)."

Clinicians often believed that lesbians needed assistance adjusting to their femininity as well as altering their sexual behavior. It was not unusual, for example, for adolescent lesbians to be sent to psychiatrists and psychologists by parents worried about a prolonged tomboy phase in their daughters or a suspiciously close friendship with another girl. Once in therapy, professionals encouraged their patients to indulge in sexual fantasies about men or even enter relationships with them, since what they needed to do was conquer their fears of heterosexual intercourse. Therapists concentrated their efforts on making their lesbian patients look and act more feminine, as if makeup and high heels would guarantee instant heterosexuality. One lesbian recalled that her therapist instructed her to start wearing skirts while she was under hypnosis!

9

Off the Couches,
into the Streets

THE ATTACK ON "CURES" was more than a matter of
personal witness. It was a political crusade that gained
momentum with every passing year during the 1960s
and reached its peak between the Stonewall riots in
1969 and the 1973 vote by the American Psychiatric
Association to remove homosexuality from its official
list of mental disturbances. Supported and energized
by the visibility of people who took the risk to "come
out," gay men and women denied that the pain they
felt was personal and rejected the language of sickness
in favor of a much more political vocabulary. Gay was
good. Homophobia was the enemy.

As early as 1964, Mattachine activist Randy Wicker
protested the role played by psychological experts in
promoting homophobia when he picketed a panel of
psychoanalysts speaking at Cooper Union in New
York City. According to a fellow activist, he announced: "Stop talking about us and let us talk for

*Held on June 27, 1982,
the 10th annual San
Francisco Lesbian/Gay
Freedom Day Parade
was touted at the time
as the largest one-day
gathering of gays and
lesbians ever. The parade
was the culmination of a
decade's worth of political
protest and organizing
by activists.*

ourselves." His request that gay people be given equal time was ignored, but Wicker's action attracted a lot of attention and encouraged others to step up the pressure on professional helpers.

Professional meetings of physicians, psychologists, and specialists in "behavior modification" were just a few of the targets of so-called zap actions in the years that followed. Often allied with feminist activists (who had their own long list of complaints about how psychological experts treated women), groups of gay men and lesbians went well beyond the polite picketing that Wicker had pioneered. They boldly interrupted professional gatherings, rattled the nerves of experts who liked to think they had all the answers, and presented demands for radical changes. Clever slogans were coined and imaginative flyers were written for these events. "We interrupt this program of psychiatric propaganda to bring you a message from Gay Pride," declared one group of spirited activists. For good measure, they added: "Off the Couches, Into the Streets!"

Psychoanalysts who had peddled cures were the first, most logical objects of activist anger because their views were so dogmatic and yet so popular at the same time. A 1968 American Medical Association talk by Charles Socarides was picketed by activists who called for gay-positive views to be represented at future conferences. That same year, a psychiatric forum on homosexuality at Columbia University's College of Physicians and Surgeons prompted a demonstration by members of the campus homophile group. They demanded "to be participants in considerations of our condition and in the disposition of our fate. It is time that talk stopped being about us and started being with us."

Irving Bieber ("one of the worst mind-pigs") was zapped in 1970, one year after Stonewall. A bearded male activist named Konstantin, wearing a bright red dress, grabbed a microphone in San Francisco's Veterans Memorial Auditorium and shouted: "We've listened to you long enough; you listen to us. We're fed up with being told we're sick. You're the ones who are sick. We're gay and we're proud." He and his fellow protesters demanded nothing less than "the abolition of psychiatry as an oppressive tool." In a few short years, the hope that psychological experts might enlighten the public and lead the way toward a

Sylvia Rivera (left) and Bebe Scarpi, members of the radical Gay Liberation Front (GLF), demonstrate at New York City's Bellevue Hospital in 1970. The GLF insisted that "the personal is political" and regarded sexual liberation as an integral part of societal transformation.

better future had evaporated almost completely. Anti–Bieber protester Gary Alinder remembers thinking that "the shrinks don't know their elbows from their assholes." He even called Bieber a "motherfucker" to his face. Needless to say, the experts were shocked. One psychiatrist even demanded that police be called in to shoot the disorderly intruders.

Psychoanalysts were not the only experts who invited public ridicule. In 1970, a national conference devoted to behavior modification was disrupted during a screening of a film on aversive conditioning with indignant chants of "medieval torture" and "barbarism." In 1971, a broadcast interview with David Reuben, author of the best-selling *Everything You Always Wanted to Know About Sex but Were Afraid to*

Ask, was turned upside down by furious protesters who accused him of homophobia. Even fictional characters such as the lead character of television's popular dramatic series "Marcus Welby, M.D." were mocked in public. The Gay Activist Alliance organized a sit-in at the offices of ABC to object to the show's portrayal of gay people as "guilt-ridden mental cases." "Marcus Welby is a Quack," the demonstrators charged, "and a Bigot!"

How gay men and lesbians felt about themselves—or at least what they said about themselves—during these years changed very quickly. What psychological experts had to say about them, on the other hand, changed slowly, if at all. One result was that the very same clinical literature that had allowed earlier generations to recognize themselves and one another prompted only disgust among gay men and lesbians who came of age during the late 1960s. Shirley Willer, eventually elected as national president of Daughters of Bilitis, recalled that in the 1940s, "I discovered I was gay . . . sitting in a classroom in nursing school in Chicago, listening to a lecture on mental hygiene." For Willer, it was a significant moment of self-realization. In contrast, Jeanne Cordova, who was a college student in 1970, remembers that

> the day I discovered that my Cal State Abnormal Psych text called me "gender dysfunctional," I brought my text home. In a furious burst of rare culinary endeavor, I flung butter into a frying pan and threw Abnormal Psych on the burner. Moments later, Judy came flying out of the bedroom, gasping "What's that horrible smell?"
>
> "I'm sending Abnormal Psych back to hell where it belongs," I answered calmly, spatula in hand. "I'm frying this heresy like a good Catholic."

Responses like Cordova's and the zap actions of the 1960s revealed just how much disrespect and frustration had been building up among gay activists. Science was hardly a guarantee of neutrality and enlightenment, as many gay men and lesbians had once believed. It might even be a convenient cover for old-fashioned prejudice.

Just as pivotal as the unscientific tilt of psychoanalysis was the electrified political landscape of the late 1960s. The single most important lesson that gay activists learned from the various nationalist, feminist, and peace movements of the day was probably that genuine change resulted from masses of people speaking out and standing up for themselves. Experts could not be trusted to engineer understanding and acceptance on the basis of disinterested information. When it came to their own experience, gay men and lesbians—not scientific authorities—were the real experts. Only they could improve their own lives.

The militance of gay activists in the late 1960s seemed light-years away from the cautious campaign for toleration that homophile organizations had mounted just a few years earlier. Self-acceptance, self-esteem, and other indicators of mental health were still central aims, though, even if no one expected the experts to deliver them. "We homosexuals of gay liberation believe that the adjustment school of therapy is not a valid approach to society," read a leaflet that members of Chicago Gay Liberation distributed at the 1970 meetings of the American Medical Association.

> We refuse to adjust to our oppression, and believe that the key to our mental health, and to the mental health of all oppressed peoples in a racist, sexist, capitalist society, is a radical change in the structure and accompanying attitudes of the entire social system. . . . We furthermore urge psychiatrists to refer their homosexual patients to gay liberation. . . . We are convinced that a picket and a dance will do more for the vast majority of homosexuals than two years on the couch.

Coming to emotional terms with one's sexual orientation and finding peace of mind were still crucial, and gay support groups and community organizations proliferated for exactly these purposes. "Our first job is to liberate ourselves," declared one of the most widely circulated manifestos of gay liberation, "and that means clearing our heads of the garbage that's been poured into them."

Only the source of psychological insight and freedom had changed. Consciousness-raising and political involvement might bring salvation, even if science and psychotherapy no longer could.

Diagnostic and Statistical Manual of Mental Disorders

(Third Edition - Revised)

DSM-III-R

American Psychiatric Association

10

The Political Career of a Diagnosis

The Diagnostic and Statistical Manual of Mental Disorders is the American Psychiatric Association's official handbook of diagnostic criteria. In the early 1970s, this seemingly innocuous scientific tome was the focus of a bitter struggle between gay and lesbian activists and the psychiatric establishment.

BETWEEN 1970 AND 1973, the front line of the war between the gay movement and organized psychological expertise was in the American Psychiatric Association (APA), which had a long-standing habit of discussing homosexuality only under the headings of "perversion" and "sexual deviation." The battle was over homosexuality's status as a diagnosis. Should it remain classified as a type of mental disturbance, be modified in some way, or be eliminated altogether from the second edition of the *Diagnostic and Statistical Manual of Psychiatric Disorders,* known as *DSM-II?*

Irving Bieber's nasty confrontation with gay and lesbian activists at the 1970 meetings in San Francisco worried the APA's program planners. In hopes of avoiding a clash the next year, they agreed to schedule a session in which homosexuals would talk about their own lives. In May 1971, for the first time in its history, the APA allowed gay men and lesbians to speak for themselves on a panel titled "Lifestyles of Non-Patient Homosexuals." (Participants dubbed it "Lifestyles of *Im*-Patient Homosexuals.") The panelists were Frank Kameny, the prominent leader of the Washington, D.C., Mattachine Society; Larry Littlejohn of the Society for Individual Rights in San Francisco; Del Martin, a founder of Daughters of Bilitis; Lilli Vincenz, a lesbian activist; and Jack Baker, student body president at the University of Minnesota.

For many gay activists, this small step did not prove that compromise with the experts was the best way to make progress. Rather, it proved just the opposite. Their disruptive tactics of the year before had worked and should definitely be used again. Frank Kameny, for example, backed a strategy that combined feisty public confrontation with give-and-take behind the scenes. During the 1960s, Kameny had emerged as one of the gay community's most articulate critics of psychiatric authority, and he spoke on the historic 1971 panel. As a scientist himself, Kameny was accustomed to looking beneath the surface of technical jargon and examining the validity of experimental methods. His training prepared him to point out the scientific inadequacy of terms such as "pathology," "sickness," and "disorder," and scold researchers for their poor sampling techniques. "This entire 'sickness theory' of homosexuality is shabby, shoddy, slipshod, slovenly, sleazy, and just-plain-bad science," he concluded. Although Kameny's appeal to the scientific conscience of APA members probably helped to persuade some, others held fast to their traditional opinions. "Dr. Kameny's polemics will not remove his inferiority feelings," condescendingly sniffed Dr. Bernard J. Pipe of Seattle, Washington.

In a move that showed gay activists were willing to work on all available fronts, Kameny also participated enthusiastically in the rowdy conference disruption, which had been planned well in advance. "Psychiatry is the enemy incarnate," Kameny shouted into a microphone during the APA's solemn Convocation of Fellows on May 3. "Psychiatry has waged a relentless war of extermination against us. You may take this as a declaration of war against you." Activists also stormed the convention display hall, where they threatened to destroy a booth marketing the tools of aversive conditioning if the offending exhibit was not immediately dismantled. There was more than enough outrage to go around. Some psychiatrists, appalled at these intimidating tactics, compared gay activists to Nazis.

By the end of the 1971 convention, gay activists had focused their fury on a single demand. Homosexuality had to be removed from the APA's list of psychiatric disorders. Preparations for the next annual APA conference included a display, "Gay, Proud, and Healthy: The Homosexual Community Speaks," intended to win over psychiatric allies to the cause of deleting homosexuality from the *DSM-II*. "We had pictures of loving gay couples . . . and the word love in great big red letters," according to organizer Barbara Gittings. And there was yet another panel—"Psychiatry—Friend or Foe to Homosexuals?"—that brought gay activists (Frank Kameny and Barbara Gittings) together with sympathetic APA members (Robert Seidenberg and Judd Marmor). Kameny toned down his criticism somewhat, Gittings quoted the moving testimony of closeted psychiatrists, and Marmor and Seidenberg appealed to the professional pride of their colleagues: "The cruelty, the thoughtlessness, the lack of common humanity, in the attitudes reflected by many conservative psychiatrists is . . . a disgrace to our profession." It was the first time that members of the APA had so publicly criticized their own organization on behalf of homosexuals.

The most dramatic moment, however, was undoubtedly the appearance of "Dr. H. Anonymous" (John Fryer) on the panel, dressed in a full rubber mask, a wig, and an extra large tuxedo to hide his identity. A special microphone also distorted his voice. "I am a homosexual. I am a psychiatrist," declared the disguised doctor to 500 of his colleagues. "My greatest loss is my honest humanity. How incredible that we homosexual psychiatrists cannot be honest in a profession that calls itself compassionate and 'helping.'" The audience was stunned. Many had never considered that members of their own profession might be gay or lesbian. According to Dr. H. Anonymous, whose presence on the panel was the brainchild of Philadelphia lesbian activist Kay Lahusen, an underground social network of homosexuals had existed within the APA for years. It included more than 200 psychiatrists. They called themselves the Gay-PA.

The bureaucratic process of revising the *DSM*, which required approval by the APA Board of Trustees, was already well underway in

the APA's Committee on Nomenclature when Robert Spitzer of the New York State Psychiatric Institute, a member of the nomenclature committee, came into contact with gay activists for the first time after the 1972 meetings. Impressed by their intelligence as well as their passion, he invited Ronald Gold of the New York Gay Activist Alliance

Gay activists take to the street in Albany, New York, in March 1971. Like many other elements of American society, the medical establishment was reluctant to concede that same-sex orientation was not necessarily an indication of maladjustment or illness.

to organize a formal presentation for the committee's consideration, and he agreed to sponsor yet another APA panel, this one devoted specifically to the question of whether homosexuality should remain in the *DSM.*

Ironically, none of the members of the committee charged with evaluating psychiatry's diagnostic categories were either strong supporters or opponents of the change. Few had done any clinical work with homosexuals, and most knew nothing about homosexuality at all. Charles Silverstein, a clinical psychologist with the Institute for Human Identity, a gay counseling center in New York, prepared a statement for the meeting with the APA committee on February 8, 1973, drawing creatively from the psychiatric literature on homosexuality and seeking the input of supportive experts. Wardell Pomeroy, one of Alfred Kinsey's original collaborators, was recruited to help, and he wrote to the APA committee: "I have high hopes that even psychiatry can profit by its mistakes and can proudly enter the last quarter of the twentieth century." The psychiatric profession had managed to ignore Kinsey's findings for 25 years, Pomeroy implied scornfully, but it was better to correct mistakes late than never.

In his presentation to the committee, Silverstein made the kind of argument that was most likely to persuade a group of psychiatrists. He talked their language. He was analytic. He was comprehensive. He was professional. Instead of expressing indignation about the persecution of gay men and lesbians, he stressed what a major scientific error it would be to continue classifying homosexuality as a mental illness. Silverstein reviewed a mass of research findings, pointed out that several psychiatrists with national reputations opposed homosexuality's inclusion in the *DSM,* and characterized the views of figures like Bieber and Socarides as "subjective and undocumented theories" that amounted to "adult (fairy) tales." "It is no sin to have made an error in the past," he informed the committee, "but surely you will mock the principles of scientific research upon which the diagnostic system is based if you turn your backs on the only objective evidence we have."

The meeting was a great success. Committee members, previously uncommitted on the question of homosexuality, expressed real willingness to consider change. Opponents of change quickly organized an Ad Hoc Committee Against the Deletion of Homosexuality from DSM-II. By May 1973, when the annual APA meetings were held in Honolulu, the entire professional association was in an uproar over the issue of homosexuality. It had become the single most controversial issue facing the profession of psychiatry—a "hot potato."

Approximately 1,000 psychiatrists attended the session that Spitzer had organized to air all sides of the issue. The mood was tense. The speakers were sharply divided. Bieber and Socarides argued for the traditional view: homosexuality was a curable mental illness caused in early childhood by pathological parenting. "Removal of the term from the manual would be tantamount to an official declaration by the APA that homosexuality is normal," Bieber warned. And making homosexuality normal would mean abandoning agonized patients and psychiatry's long history of humanitarianism, both unforgivable acts. Heterosexual behavior and orientation, Socarides added, "are basic to elementary human biology and are not subject to change by social or political movements." Judd Marmor, a psychoanalyst who had been one of the first well-known psychiatrists to renounce the sickness theory, strongly urged deletion. He reviewed the growing body of empirical research on "normal" homosexuals and called upon his colleagues to do their professional duty. "If our judgment about the mental health of heterosexuals were based only on those whom we see in our clinical practices we would have to conclude that all heterosexuals are also mentally ill," he pointed out. "It is our task as psychiatrists to be healers of the distressed, not watchdogs of our social mores."

Ronald Gold was the only gay activist on the 1973 APA panel. He described his own destructive contacts with psychiatrists and their cures, beginning at age 14 and ending in the famous Menninger Clinic. "I have come to an unshakable conclusion," he said. "The illness theory of homosexuality is a pack of lies. . . . Psychiatry—dedicated to making sick people well—has been the cornerstone of a system of oppression that makes people sick." Gold described how his feelings of self-doubt and disgust had disappeared after he came out and reported that his work and love life were both much happier. "Would you rather have me the way I am?" he sarcastically asked the auditorium full of psychiatrists. "Or would you suggest another round of therapy?"

Finally, Robert Spitzer proposed a change that offered something to both sides in the debate. He suggested that heterosexuality was "optimal" and that homosexuality was "suboptimal." But even as "an irregular form of sexual behavior," homosexuality did not meet the requirements for being classified as a mental illness, according to Spitzer, since many homosexuals were well-functioning people who felt little or no distress about their sexual orientation. Those who were uncomfortable with their homosexuality, however, deserved psychiatric attention and assistance. He concluded by proposing that homosexuality be deleted from the *DSM* and replaced by a new classification, "Sexual Orientation Disturbance."

"This is for people whose sexual interests are directed primarily toward people of the same sex and who are bothered by, in conflict with, or wish to change their sexual orientation. Such a diagnostic category is distinguished from homosexuality, which by itself does not constitute a psychiatric disorder." Spitzer reassured the large audience that approving this change did not mean that the APA was taking any particular position on the cause or desirability of homosexuality. Deleting homosexuality from the *DSM* would not make it "normal" or equal to heterosexuality. Psychiatry was not caving in to gay activism.

On December 15, 1973, the APA Board of Trustees finally met and decided to remove homosexuality and replace it with "Sexual Orientation Disturbance," exactly as Spitzer had recommended. The trustees also passed a strongly worded civil rights resolution, putting the APA on record against discrimination in employment, housing, and public accommodations and in favor of new legislation, at all levels of government, to protect the legal rights of homosexuals.

Gay activists celebrated the deletion as a major, if long overdue, victory. "I was thrilled," Barbara Gittings said. "The APA decision took an enormous burden off our backs." Then she added, "We were cured overnight by the stroke of a pen." Sarcastic humor was common among gay men and lesbians who appreciated psychiatry's cultural power to define homosexuality as much as they resented it. "Twenty million homosexuals gain instant cure!" announced Philadelphia's gay community newspaper. It was hard to tell whether the headline was more a delighted cheer or contemptuous howl. Howard Brown of the National Gay Task Force, respectable physician though he was, commented that "the board's vote made millions of Americans who had been officially ill that morning officially well that afternoon. Never in history had so many people been cured in so little time."

The APA decision, however, did not bring the dispute within the association to an end. Almost as soon as the trustees acted, the professional association was engulfed in controversy once again. Led by Bieber and Socarides, opponents of homosexuality's deletion from the *DSM* mobilized to put the change to the test of an association-wide vote. They charged that the APA Board had perpetrated "the medical hoax of the century" and acted against the scientific evidence as well as the convictions of a majority of psychiatrists. According to one irate APA member, "I think the Board of Trustees did not have the strength and guts to resist superficial social pressure from homosexuals who, having a collective Oedipal complex, wish to destroy the American Psychiatric Association. It is a bad day for psychiatry."

Over 10,000 psychiatrists participated in the referendum. It showed that no clear consensus existed on homosexuality's psychiatric status: 58 percent favored the board's decision and 37 percent opposed it. Since almost 4 out of 10 APA members polled agreed with the view that homosexuality constituted a mental illness, the removal of homosexuality from the *DSM* could not be taken as a sign that psychiatry as a whole had changed. On the other hand, the fact that a significant majority of APA members favored the change did indicate that the old analytic perspective no longer exerted a stranglehold on the profession. The days of "arrested development" and mother-blame were numbered. Unanimity that homosexuality was a "condition" had been shattered for good.

11

Backlash

AFTER 1973, PSYCHIATRIC ALLIES of the gay community moved slowly but surely into positions of power within the APA. One after another, APA presidents made speeches calling for an end to the discriminatory policies of school boards, the U.S. military, and the Immigration and Naturalization Service. Advocates of the illness theory, on the other hand, were enraged by their diminished clout. They stepped up the rhetoric and exerted pressure to reverse the change, but to no avail. The new diagnosis, "Sexual Orientation Disturbance," sparked debate for several more years, appeared in the 1980 edition of the *DSM* as "Ego-Dystonic Homosexuality" (much to the dismay of gay and lesbian psychiatrists and activists), and then was quietly removed altogether in 1986. The very same establishment that had for so long given its blessings to curing homosexuality now counts itself a fast friend of the gay community.

Marchers in the 15th annual Gay Pride parade in New York City pass by St. Patrick's Cathedral on their way down Fifth Avenue. The placard refers to Cardinal (then archbishop) John O'Connor, head of the Roman Catholic Diocese of New York and an outspoken opponent of gay rights.

Leaders of organized psychiatry are friendlier today than they have ever been before, and many more psychological experts have dedicated themselves to the task of supporting gay men and lesbians in their struggle against oppression and invisibility. On balance, the change has been both dramatic and positive, but the old attitudes have not been wiped away for good. Since 1973, backlash has been brewing, which is not that surprising considering that the general political climate in the country has tilted sharply toward conservative social views. Four years after the fateful decision, a poll of the APA membership revealed that a majority of psychiatrists had not changed their minds. Sixty-nine percent thought that homosexuality was usually pathological; only 18 percent disagreed. Sixty percent considered homosexuals less capable of loving, emotionally stable relationships than heterosexuals. In 1978, another survey illustrated that medical education and residency programs had barely noticed the deletion of homosexuality from the *DSM*. Only five percent of the programs that trained future psychiatrists reported presenting homosexuality as a normal type of human sexuality. Not surprisingly, many standard textbooks in psychiatry and psychology persisted in presenting homosexuality as a pathological condition. There had been a lot of turmoil over changing the diagnosis. Was anything really that different?

Heartened by the socially conservative climate ushered in by Ronald Reagan's presidential election in 1980, leaders of the old guard dusted off their tried-and-true themes, certain that public opinion was with them and not behind the APA leadership. "The suspicion with which middle America views homosexuality cannot be voted out of existence," remarked well-known psychoanalyst Abram Kardiner. He went on to predict that homosexuality, and the general crisis in sexual identity provoked by women's demand for equality, would together destroy American civilization. "The loss of sexual identity makes man a rudderless ship with a cargo of dynamite," he warned ominously in 1978. Even more remarkable than Kardiner's exaggerated rhetoric was the fact that psychoanalytic thinking about homosexuality stubbornly resisted most of the dramatic changes that came in the wake of gay liberation. It was stuck in the past and seemed uninterested in the future.

So was the popular press and public opinion. Both held fast to the sickness view, unwilling to swallow the APA's turnabout. Ann Landers, whose advice column is read by millions, always considered herself a champion of gay rights. But in 1976, she wrote that "I do not believe homosexuality is 'just another life style.' I believe these people suffer from a severe personality disorder. Granted some are sicker than others, but sick they are and all the fancy rhetoric of the American Psychiatric Association will not change it." Many Americans apparently agreed. In 1985, after HIV had been identified and AIDS was beginning to get press coverage as a major health issue, a poll by the *Los Angeles Times* found that 79 percent of its national sample believed that homosexuality was wrong.

Neither did the advocates of cure fade away entirely after 1973. During the 1980s, promises of conversion to heterosexuality were still made by a few sexologists, but usually for new reasons. William Masters and Virginia Johnson, America's most famous sex experts and prophets of a sex-is-good ethic, expressed the view that "homosexuality in contemporary society is a viable life style." They would never have dreamed of saying that it was sick or immoral, but they maintained that gay men and lesbians troubled by their sexual feelings had the right to individual choice in the matter. Altering sexual orientation implied nothing about the intrinsic worth of homosexuality, according to them, even though no heterosexual clients came calling who wished to make the opposite choice.

The Masters and Johnson Institute offered "dissatisfied homosexual men" a treatment program custom-designed to introduce them to the mysterious ways of the opposite sex and alleviate anxieties about finding dates, making eye contact with women, and touching unfamiliar body parts. The therapy revolved around two weeks of complete isolation with a member of the opposite sex, during which men brushed up on basic social skills and tried to get comfortable with verbal and sexual interaction. "Therapy for homosexuals who want reorientation is a controversial topic," Masters and Johnson freely admitted. "However, to ignore the goals of clients who want to change their preference is both paradoxical and prejudiced." Cure had become simply a personal

Ushered in by the election of Ronald Reagan (right) as president of the United States, the decade of the 1980s was a period of increased political and social conservatism that threatened to reverse many of the gains of the gay civil rights movement. This rise of conservatism was aided by the growth of the fundamentalist Christian movement as a political force, which enabled evangelists such as the Reverend Jerry Falwell (left) to gain a national following.

makeover, a commodity in the free market of therapeutic self-transformation.

In the 1970s and 1980s, many Protestant and Jewish denominations gradually liberalized their policies toward homosexuality and homosexuals, a change that was at once extremely important, very welcome, and long overdue. Nevertheless, some Catholics and fundamentalist Christians took up the banner of cure, and in the new era of gay freedom, they probably attracted more attention than their small numbers warranted. In 1973, Love in Action became one of the first ministries established for the specific purpose of converting homosexuals to heterosexuality. In 1977, Anita Bryant, a born-again entertainer, kicked off a major antigay crusade (called Save Our Children) in Dade County, Florida, that included plans for a counseling center set up to persuade gay men and women to mend their ways by accepting Christ. Courage, a Catholic organization with branches in fifteen urban dioceses, advocates strict chastity. It encourages homosexuals to "live chaste lives in accordance with the Roman Catholic church's teaching on homosexuality" and "live lives that may serve as good examples to other homosexuals." Homosexuality is a learned sin, these groups believe, and it can be unlearned with a little bit of divine help.

Exodus International, a fundamentalist group founded in 1976, has devoted itself to "helping people who desire recovery from sexual brokenness." This particular "recovery," of course, must be found in religious salvation. Exodus tries to "communicate the message of liberation from homosexuality through repentance and faith in Jesus Christ as Savior and Lord." Emboldened by the growth of the New Christian Right and the support of the Reagan and Bush administrations during the 1980s, Exodus makes the astonishing claim that 71.6 percent of homosexuals can become heterosexual if they really wish to do so.

Born-again cures all assumed that change was necessary because homosexuality was sinful and contrary to the will of God, but Christians did not hesitate to recruit like-minded mental health professionals to their cause. Individuals like William P. Wilson, head of biological psychiatry at Duke University Medical Center, added a touch of expert legitimacy to a patently religious campaign:

> Treatment using dynamic individual psychotherapy, group therapy, aversion therapy, or psychotherapy with an integration of Christian principles will produce object choice reorientation and successful heterosexual relationships in a high percentage of persons. . . . Homosexuals can change their sexual orientation. God has condemned homosexual behavior and has made the power to change available to those who desire it. Therefore, "homosexual and Christian" is a contradiction. Homosexuals have no excuse, but if they desire change, they do have hope.

Fundamentalists also borrowed healing techniques (therapy as well as prayer) and psychoanalytic lingo when they thought it would help their case. Elizabeth Moberly, a therapist affiliated with Exodus, has appeared on numerous television talk shows, explaining that homosexuality is what happens when boys will be girls and girls will be boys. What she is saying is pretty much what physicians a century ago said about sexual inversion, with a few Freudian concepts thrown in. Homosexuality is caused by a "radical disidentification from the parent of the same sex," which leads to "a defensive detachment from the same-sex love-source and a reparative striving for a restored attachment." Lesbians and gay men are the way they are because their parents have made them "psychological orphans" who just cannot come to terms with being masculine men and feminine women. Since "normal" gender identification is a necessary step in developing a "hetero-psychologic personality structure," homosexuality, Moberly argues, can be prevented with a little more attention to gender-appropriate childhood activities. Football can do wonders for boys. For girls, sewing will do the trick.

Cures have taken secular forms in recent years as well. Psychologist Joseph Nicolosi is the spokesperson for the fairly new National Association for Research and Therapy of Homosexuality, which boasts a membership of more than 300. Nicolosi does not allow religion to interfere with his mission of transforming gay men who hate themselves into happy husbands and loving fathers. Like Exodus, and just like the psychoanalysts of the 1950s and 1960s, Nicolosi's position is that male homosexuality is "a developmental problem" and not as valid a form of sexual expression as male heterosexuality. Failure to learn correct gender identification in childhood can be fixed by clinicians trained in the intricacies of "reparative therapy," which aims to repair the mutilated bond between father and son. This therapy "acknowledges the significance of gender difference, the worth of family and conventional values, and the importance of the prevention of gender confusion in children." Nicolosi claims that by subscribing to the idea of the happy homosexual, most of his professional colleagues have surrendered their moral obligation to help people in pain. These miserable people, whom Nicolosi calls "non-gay homosexuals," need the help that reparative therapy can offer. The American Psychiatric Association disagrees on the grounds that such therapy does not work. An official statement, dated April 1993, reads: "There is no published scientific evidence of 'reparative therapy' as a treatment to change one's sexual orientation." In spite of pressure from lesbian and gay psychiatrists to go further, the APA has still not voted to condemn such practices as unethical.

Nicolosi's is not the only variation on the old theme of the analytic fix. Dr. Robert Kronemeyer advanced a kind of "new age" version of the idea that homosexuality is disturbed, pathetic, and less than completely human. Meditation, breathing exercises, and a diet without caffeine and sugar were all steps on the road to emotional self-help, and Kronemeyer claimed that he could help four out of five homosexuals free themselves from sexual abnormality. On top of all their other

After the death of Alfred Kinsey, the husband-and-wife team of William Masters and Virginia Johnson became the best-known researchers of sexual behavior in the United States. Though insisting that a homosexual orientation should carry no stigma, Masters and Johnson nonetheless offered in their clinics "reorientation therapy" for "dissatisfied homosexual men."

problems, Kronemeyer pointed out that most gay people also suffered from severe sleeping disorders! His technique, called syntonic therapy, worked by taking people back to the experiences that had damaged them as infants and encouraging them to get mad—almost always at their mothers.

The details of Kronemeyer's cure were designed for the 1980s, but the underlying theory went back to the 1950s. "Homosexuality is a pathological adaptation to a damaged and twisted early environment," especially a "disturbed infant-mother relationship," he claimed. His recipe for "overcoming homosexuality" included therapy for all mem-

Anti-gay demonstrators express their opinion during the 1984 Gay Pride parade in New York City. Many homophobes continue to cite the scriptural authority of the Bible as justification for their bias while willfully ignoring the New Testament's message of tolerance and compassion.

bers of the family and a stay-at-home-mom for every single child in America. Like the experts from earlier periods, he claimed to be a compassionate helper with nothing but sympathy for the suffering victims. In the 1980s, cures were still recommended for homosexuals' own good. Homosexuality spelled misery. Heterosexuality guaranteed happiness.

Even institutionalization has not entirely vanished as a cure, especially for adolescents. Recently, the National Center for Lesbian Rights (NCLR) has gathered 20 reports of gay teens being locked up and subjected to the familiar old treatments of aversion, covert desensitization, and drugs, as well as "reparative therapy," the new variation on the old analytic fix. While the numbers are tiny, the trend is still worrisome. These young people, according to NCLR attorney Shannon Minter, come from all across the country and have been labeled with "borderline personality disorder," "gender identity disorder," and other diagnoses. One young woman in New York ended up in a public psychiatric ward after trying to kill herself. While she was hospitalized, she was locked in an isolation room and told that she could not be trusted around other girls because of her lesbianism. Similarly, a Hawaiian teen was institutionalized and heavily sedated for a year, during which he was vigorously counseled against homosexuality.

One 17-year-old, Lynn Duff, managed to escape from a Utah facility where she had been held for six months after her mother stumbled across a love poem that Lynn had written to another girl. Today, Duff lives in San Francisco, where she has founded a new national organization, the Students and Teens Opposing Psychiatric Abuse Network. These disturbing cases illustrate that while "homosexuality" can no longer be used as a formal diagnosis, it is only the language of cure that has changed. Today, few institutions will publicly announce that their purpose is to alter homosexual orientation. Instead, they refer to "deprogramming" and "straightening out" troubled youngsters.

MY DAUGHTER
is LESBIAN
AND THAT'S OK
YOU'RE
YOU'RE
THAT'S OK
HEART
I'm Walking
WE OUR
GAY CHILDREN

12

A Psychology of Our Own

In recent years, an increasing number of parents, like these mothers who took part in the Gay Pride Festival Parade in Los Angeles, California, in 1986, have been willing to demonstrate their support for their gay or lesbian children.

WHILE A FEW PSYCHOLOGICAL experts and religious zealots were looking for ways to move forward into the past, most gay activists were busy with other tasks. After the APA's 1973 decision, gay men and lesbians were happy to be relieved of the job of constantly battling these expert enemies and turned enthusiastically toward building a psychology of their very own.

Some of the first tentative steps in this new direction were taken by gay men and lesbians who were helping professionals themselves. Almost entirely closeted before 1973, these experts began coming out and forming open caucuses within their professional organizations. The secret social group within the APA to which Dr. H. Anonymous had referred—the Gay-PA—came out publicly in 1975 as the Lesbian, Gay, and Bisexual Caucus.

Nonpsychiatric professionals had moved faster. The independent Association of Lesbian and Gay Psychologists was formed at the meetings of the American Psychological Association in 1973 and, in January 1975, that organization took a position that was more far-reaching than the *DSM* change. First, the American Psychological Association rejected the sickness theory of homosexuality. Then, it pledged itself (and urged others) to work actively against antigay prejudice:

> Homosexuality, per se, implies no impairment in judgment, stability, reliability, or general social or vocational capabilities: Further, the American Psychological Association urges all mental health professionals to take the lead in removing the stigma of mental illness that has long been associated with homosexual orientations.

In addition to providing an internal network of support to gays and lesbians, these professional interest groups took up the challenge of monitoring activities related to gay and lesbian issues and pressing their parent organizations to actively promote a civil rights agenda. Today, groups of this sort exist not only among psychiatrists and psychologists but in the National Association of Social Workers, the American Association for Marriage and Family Therapy, and the American Association of Sex Educators, Counselors, and Therapists. An independent National Association for Lesbian and Gay Alcoholism Professionals draws members from a number of different helping professions.

Peer counseling, whose mission was to provide supportive psychological services, typically by nonprofessionals, was a key element of the post-Stonewall gay movement from the very first. Identity House in New York, the Homophile Clinic in Boston, and the Gay Community Services Center in Los Angeles were only three of the community institutions that offered peer counseling, completely free of charge. The expense of professional therapy was not the only thing keeping gay men and lesbians away from it in the 1970s, however. The formally trained experts who had so recently tried to cure them of their "condition" did not appear to be trustworthy allies, regardless of the actions their professional organizations had taken. In 1973, the best-selling women's health manual *Our Bodies, Ourselves* titled its discussion of lesbians and psychiatry "The Rapists" and warned readers "to be wary of psychiatrists and analysts—that is, therapists with medical training—as that branch of the psych field that is the most reactionary." Lesbian activist Karla Jay put it even more bluntly. Therapists are "a flock of rip-off artists in our very midst. Don't give your head to just anyone." Take your time. Shop around.

But even in the 1970s, there were signs that gay-friendly psychotherapy was destined for great success. Many younger lesbians embraced the alternative "feminist therapy" they had first encountered in the women's movement in the form of small group consciousness-raising. Instead of telling their clients to shave their legs and do something with their hair, feminist therapists actually supported questions about sex-role stereotypes. The problem was not with women but with society, and it was liberating to finally have therapists say so. After decades of being lectured (mainly by men) about the dangers of turning away from conventional femininity, women were relieved to find that their therapists were finally complaining too. Not all feminist therapists were acquainted with lesbians, of course, or supportive of them, but feminist therapy was still a huge improvement. Lesbians flocked to it, and many became therapists themselves.

By 1980 or so, a post-Stonewall cohort had gone through school and entered the mental health professions. For these gay men and lesbians, the decision to become helpers, indeed their very professional identities, were wrapped up in the desire to conduct gay-positive research, formulate gay-positive theory, and provide gay-positive clinical services. Their new visibility in the mental health fields, combined with increasing demands for respectful service delivery to gay individuals and communities, has resulted in a more pluralistic and less judgmental understanding of psychosexual development. Inspired by tremendously creative feminist work on the psychology of gender identity, entirely new definitions of mature sexual expression, healthy gender development, and mental well-being have been constructed.

The ultimate goal was to put psychology permanently on the side of the gay community. Today, gay and lesbian experts with interests in a wide variety of fields are proud that "a gay-affirmative perspective has emerged within American psychology." New journals, like the *Journal of Gay and Lesbian Psychotherapy,* which began publishing in 1989, appear regularly, as do specialized societies devoted to gay and lesbian experience, such as Division 44 of the American Psychological Association and the Society for the Psychological Study of Lesbian and Gay Issues. Psychological experts have attempted to educate the U.S. Supreme Court about the centrality of sexual freedom to mental health. They have scrutinized the attitudes of their colleagues on a range of issues affecting gay men and lesbians. They have made suggestions for eliminating bias in psychological research and language. Clinical education, though still too often silent on homosexuality, is nevertheless much more likely than in the past to include some mention of homophobia and some discussion of the psychological issues most relevant to gay men and lesbians, including their need for supportive, nonjudgmental therapists. Many students in the helping professions today are exposed to a range of gay social service organizations in the course of their training.

By all accounts, large numbers of experts now see homosexuality as a viable and healthy orientation and blame many of the problems associated with gay and lesbian life on antigay prejudice and social policy, rather than on homosexuality itself. "Changing the attitudes of an entire society is a major undertaking," commented psychologists Stephen Morin and Esther Rothblum in a recent issue of the *American Psychologist,* "and there is much reason to be proud of psychology's contribution to this effort." Even Frank Kameny, that old foe of the psychiatric establishment, agrees that psychological authority no longer poses a serious threat to the gay community. "There is nothing to be maintained by keeping an enemy. Once you have made your point, you can bring them in as allies."

During the past 15 years, gay-affirmative approaches have posed entirely new questions about the gay and lesbian experience. Often pioneered by gay men and lesbians, these approaches have found a receptive audience among heterosexual professionals as well. Instead of asking why men and women become homosexual, experts have set out to explore the diversity of gay experience, taking it as a given, rather than something in need of explanation. Experts still concentrate the bulk of their resources on gay men, but research on different phases of the lesbian life cycle has become somewhat more visible. Work has been done on everything from lesbians' career development and work behavior to lesbians in midlife and old age, problems within lesbian relationships, and the logic of eating disorders among lesbians. In many of these cases, what experts have learned about lesbian lives is entirely new. Researchers in the past were usually so obsessed with sexual orientation and behavior that they entirely overlooked basic questions about work, aging, relationships, and health.

Not every aspect of gay life has been newly discovered during the past 15 years. Gay-affirmative psychological approaches have also helped to make old subjects appear much more "normal." Lesbian motherhood is a case in point. Not that long ago, lesbian mothers were interesting to researchers mainly because of fights over child custody. Since judges had absorbed the idea that homosexuality was a mental illness, it was not unusual for them to consider women unfit mothers for no other reason than simply because they were lesbians. When psychologists and psychiatrists appeared as expert witnesses, their role was to explain what caused homosexuality in general and not to illuminate the details of a particular case. If lesbian mothers were pathological people, then it stood to reason that they were also pernicious parents. "Orgasm means more to them than children or anything else," concluded one Ohio judge in the early 1970s. Not that long ago, most legal rulings in lesbian custody cases assumed that growing up with a lesbian mother would damage the secure gender identity of a child. Judges tended to believe in a kind of "contagion" theory. Lesbian mothers had to be stopped before they infected their children and turned them gay.

Today, some judges are still preoccupied by these concerns, if the high-profile case of Sharon Bottoms is any indication. (Bottoms, a Virginia lesbian, lost custody of her son in 1993 when her own mother persuaded the judge that having a lesbian mother would confuse and harm the boy. The judge's ruling was recently overturned—after gay-positive psychiatrists, psychologists, and social workers all filed

Brian Batey (center) relaxes in the backyard of the home shared by his father, Frank Batey (right), and his father's companion, Craig Corbett (left), in Palm Springs, California. Following his parents' divorce, Brian had been kidnapped by his mother, who believed that Frank's homosexuality made him morally unsuited to share the custody of their son. In recent years, several highly publicized child custody cases have made the fitness of homosexuals as parents a subject of legal and public debate.

briefs taking exception to the view that lesbian mothers were unfit—and is currently being appealed.) However, recent research on lesbian mothers has concentrated on debunking the old myths and documenting how ordinary lesbian mothers actually are. Just like Evelyn Hooker's research on "normal" gay men in the 1950s, current perspectives on lesbian motherhood show that no significant differences exist between lesbian mothers and their heterosexual counterparts.

Ellen Lewin's 1993 study of lesbian mothers, for example, shows clearly that lesbians become mothers for all the same reasons that heterosexual women become mothers. No evidence exists that lesbianism either decreases parenting ability or harms children. Since being a *wanted* child is good no matter what the parents' sexual orientation, it is possible that being the son or daughter of a lesbian may be beneficial because lesbians who choose to become mothers after coming out must want children and make very deliberate plans for them. Having a lesbian mother, according to Lewin, neither shapes children's gender identity, decides their sexual orientation, nor influences their mental health one way or the other. In fact, Lewin found that motherhood defined women's lives to a much greater degree than sexual orientation did. Empirical findings such as Lewin's have been used successfully in custody cases, which only means that legal procedures are less likely to focus on lesbianism as the *only* issue than they were in the past. They have provided a rationale for positive legal innovations such as adoption by openly gay individuals and couples. Finally, they have helped focus attention on the everyday lives of lesbians and their children, which take place not primarily in courtrooms but in homes, schools, and neighborhoods.

In addition to exploring new subjects and providing new perspectives on old subjects, gay-affirmative psychology has highlighted the many differences between gay men and lesbians and within both of these groups. The variety of gay experience—the existence of many different homosexualities—is a central theme in today's gay-affirmative psychology. Again following the lead of feminist theorists and researchers, gay-affirmative experts point out that psychological identity is a multi-faceted phenomenon not reducible to any single factor. Sexual orientation is important, to be sure, but its meaning is shaped by other aspects of human identity, including gender (whether one is a man or woman), race, religion, ethnicity, and class background. Psychologists have studied Latinos and Latinas, African Americans, Asian Americans, and Native Americans, always trying to understand how diverse cultural communities have responded to homosexuality and shaped the identities of their gay and lesbian members.

Perhaps nothing indicates how far psychology has come quite as effectively as the fact that homophobia itself is now the subject of considerable attention from psychological experts. Tracking down the causes and cures for homophobia is a very far cry from the old attempts to locate the causes and cures for homosexuality. A number of experts in this new field have argued that fears of homosexuality are closely related to fears about gender, especially fears about femininity.

Men, according to this analysis, can deny a frightening part of themselves—the part that is full of emotions and desires for closeness and dependence—by attacking gay men (who are culturally associated with effeminacy) as well as women themselves. Gregory M. Herek, a president of the Association of Lesbian and Gay Psychologists in the late 1980s, has written extensively on the psychology of homophobia. He hypothesized that lashing out violently against homosexuals helps individuals clarify their personal values, gain social approval from people who matter, and build self-confidence. In his words, "antigay hostility thus functions to define who one *is* by identifying gay people as a symbol of who one is *not* and directing hostility toward them." If homophobia defines heterosexual masculinity so profoundly, then by implication serious social problems such as gay bashing cannot be eradicated with high-minded speeches and criminal penalties alone. The ultimate causes of homophobia are psychological, and the ultimate solutions to homophobia will be psychological too. A brand-new set of rules is required to guide men's lives.

A few brave souls have even attempted to push psychoanalysis in a gay-affirmative direction. Richard Isay, for example, a gay physician on the faculty of Cornell Medical College and Columbia University's Center for Psychoanalytic Training and Research, claims that a perspective on gay male sexuality as "constitutional" and "normal and growth-enhancing" is truer to Freud than the sickness-and-deviance model that bore his name during the years after World War II. Pathologizing homosexuality has also been bad for business. In the atmosphere of greater openness and pride that has existed since Stonewall, Isay points out, gay men interested in psychotherapy have voted with their feet, abandoning the analytic couch and patronizing nonanalytic healers instead. Consequently, orthodox analysts have seen few, if any, self-accepting gay patients who might challenge their idea that homosexuality is a developmental disturbance in need of change. Gay men have rejected psychoanalysis, so psychoanalysis has continued to reject gay men.

In contrast, Isay's own analytic practice is full of gay men who feel comfortable with their sexual orientation. This clinical experience has

prompted him to argue that all psychotherapists have a positive obligation to affirm their clients' homosexuality. And all gay men seeking
therapeutic assistance have a right to expect therapists who consider
them capable of complete and satisfying gay lives. Of course, the
therapists who are most inclined to feel this way today are probably gay
themselves.

His years as an analyst have also helped Isay to reformulate Freudian
theories about the origins of homosexual orientation. The wicked
mother who is responsible for producing homosexuality in her sons is
a figment of the sexist imagination, Isay writes. Empirical research has
revealed no differences between the parents of children who become
gay and those who do not. What Isay believes is clear from psychoanalysis with gay men is that their homoerotic fantasies began very early,
at age four or five. Isay considers this common pattern a clue that they
all struggled with incestuous feelings about their fathers. Youngsters
who will become gay adults do not move through a phase (Freud called
it the Oedipus complex) in which they secretly long for the parent of
the opposite sex and wish to do away with the parent of the same sex.
Instead, they take the same-sex parent as their primary sexual object.
For Isay, there is nothing "deviant" about this development at all. It is
a perfect mirror image of the developmental drama that creates heterosexuality. In this gay-positive version of psychoanalysis, homosexuality
is not a sign of arrested development. It is neither immature nor
perverse. It is not inferior to heterosexuality in any way, but exactly
equal and parallel to it.

Isay is highly critical of the tradition of cures. Efforts to change
homosexual preference are hurtful, not helpful. They erode the self-
esteem of gay men and impair the ability to engage in full, loving
relationships. Isay still believes that the Freudian legacy can offer insight
not only into the origins of male homosexuality but into the psychology
of homophobia as well, which he suggests is founded on the hatred of
women. He even uses psychoanalysis to analyze the views of Freudian
figures who have promoted the sickness theory. Their conviction that
only heterosexuality is developmentally normal "may in fact be one
way of expressing their anxiety about the passive, feminine aspects of

Because gays and lesbians are often made to feel unwelcome in churches and religious organizations, those who wish to worship have sometimes established their own congregations. With a membership of 1,000, the Cathedral of Hope Methodist Community Church in Dallas, Texas, claims to be home to the world's largest gay and lesbian congregation.

character that have contributed to their choice of vocation and their being accepted for analytic training." Gay psychoanalysts can give as good as they get!

Despite their many differences in background and opinion, Stephen Morin, Esther Rothblum, Ellen Lewin, Gregory Herek, and Richard Isay are all members of the new wave of post-Stonewall experts. Frequently gay or lesbian themselves, they have started to overturn the conventional wisdom about who homosexuals are and what their lives are like. Thanks largely to them and to a well-organized gay movement, the majority of gay men and lesbians today no longer talk the language of cure. It is now possible (at least for urban, well-educated, middle-class lesbians and gay men) to find supportive therapists, read sympathetic books about gay love and courtship, and carve out spaces in their daily lives that are genuinely free from being labeled deviant and dangerous. The evidence can be found in the numerous pages of ads for psycho-therapeutic and "healing" services that are common in gay community newspapers and typically outnumber all others in lesbian-oriented publications.

In part because psychotherapy has always appealed to more women than men, lesbians have been exceptionally eager consumers and clients. The first-ever national survey of lesbian health care, conducted in the mid-1980s, revealed that a "surprisingly high" proportion of all the lesbians surveyed had received professional counseling or psycho-therapy: 73 percent. No other demographic group on whom informa-tion is available appears quite as enthusiastic about therapy as American lesbians. Lesbians who are middle-aged and have earned advanced degrees are the likeliest to be in therapy, but they are not there alone. Race, religious affiliation, and even personal income do not affect the likelihood that lesbians will participate in therapy to any significant degree. Therapy has become a core institution in lesbian communities and a rather democratic one. Lesbians with diverse cultural backgrounds and different access to money are all quite likely to come into contact with it. Therapy, in fact, is perceived as so ubiquitous in lesbian communities across the country that it is frequently the subject of jokes. One postcard currently making the rounds of feminist and lesbian bookstores reads: "Let's have a nice long talk, like we used to before you had therapy."

Nonprofessional psychological services, such as peer counseling centers, have remained popular since the 1970s, and other forms of self-help have emerged. Twelve-step and other recovery programs for alcoholics, addicts, and codependents—such as Alcoholics Anonymous (AA) and Al-Anon—proliferated in America's gay communities during the 1980s. The only requirement for membership in these groups is a desire to stop abusing a substance (such as alcohol or narcotics) or change compulsive behavior, which might include overeating, gambling, or even having sex. (Sex and Love Addicts Anonymous is one of the newer 12-step programs.) Gay community centers and women's centers sponsor regular meetings of these groups, and observers often comment that recovery programs have "mushroomed" and "gone wild" in recent years. In the Boston area alone in the late 1980s, there were 20 official gay meetings of AA each week, and Al-Anon offered ten for gay men, two for lesbians, and one for bisexuals. Many recovery groups that are not formally designated as gay are full of lesbian and gay members. Although few of these groups are about homosexuality per se, and none take a formal position that homosexuality is sick, many gay people have chosen to meet together for the mutual support and affirmation of collective sharing.

Unlike professional "help," self-help programs do not cost anything. Nor do they dwell on analysis. They do not seek to uncover the reasons why people are addicted. Instead, they take a straightforward behavioral approach and encourage people to recognize the existence of a "higher power" that can help them cope. Like professional help, however, these groups talk the language of psychology. They emphasize that people should pay consistent attention to themselves, understand their motivations, and gain insight into their emotional experience. There is no necessary contradiction between self-help and expert assistance, and gay men and lesbians frequently take advantage of both.

13

Trouble in Paradise

NOT EVERYTHING IS PERFECT in the brave new world of gay-affirmative psychology. In 1991, the American Psychiatric Association's Committee on Lesbian and Gay Concerns released a report on bias in psychotherapy that had some surprising—and depressing—results. A four-page survey of over 2,500 APA members (the vast majority of them clinicians) revealed that actual clinical practice did not live up to the organization's stated policy that homosexuality per se should not be treated as a psychological disability. Personal knowledge of biased, inadequate, or inappropriate practice was reported by 58 percent of the experts who were polled. In comparison, only 5 percent reported "gay-affirmative" practice, and a disproportionate number of these were gay or lesbian themselves.

More than 20 years after Stonewall, many psychological experts have not yet adjusted. "I'm convinced that homosexuality is a genuine personality disorder and not merely a different way of life. Everyone that I have known socially or as a client has been a complete mess psychologically," one APA member wrote. Another offered the opinion "that homosexuality is abnormally atypical, that it results in excessive emphasis on the sexual aspects of life, and is ultimately self-defeating." One clinician even reported that she had been told by her own therapist that "lesbian feelings are the result of primitive arrested development, immature, repulsive, sick."

Today, many therapists continue to view homosexuality as pathological. The APA survey showed that many also automatically attribute emotional problems to homosexual orientation, focus on homosexual orientation when it is not relevant, and go out of their way to demean gay and lesbian experiences. "If you have a uterus," one therapist asked a female client struggling with her sexual orientation, "don't you think you should use it?" Some therapists tell their clients that they are heterosexual (whether they know it or not) and make the renunciation of homosexuality a condition of treatment. Some disclose their clients' sexual orientation without permission. Some label their clients as unfit parents. Other examples of bias are less extreme but still troubling. It is commonplace for therapists to lack understanding of gay relationships, to assume that only adults can be gay, or to interpret homosexuality as a "phase" that clients will inevitably outgrow. Many therapists have no idea what sort of prejudice gay men and lesbians face on a daily basis.

The news was not all bad. Members of the APA's Committee on Lesbian and Gay Concerns found encouraging signs of sensitive practice as well. Some therapists really *do* consider homosexuality to be a viable sexual orientation, no better or worse than heterosexuality. At the same time, these enlightened experts recognize the profound impact of homophobia and do their best to help clients develop positive identities and satisfying relationships in the face of stigma and hostility. Many are familiar with community resources and work hard to ensure that their clients take advantage of all available social services and support systems. For these therapists, at least, it is finally OK to be gay.

Ethical questions have plagued the practitioners and consumers of even the most gay-affirmative therapy, however. Because lesbians have been so loyal to psychotherapy, they have also usually been the first to criticize it. Some lesbians have gone so far as to condemn therapy altogether and call for its abolition. Celia Kitzinger and Rachel Perkins, although they are psychologists themselves, have pointed out that lesbians have completely changed their minds about psychology since the 1960s. As a practice that encourages lesbians to explore the psychological interior, it necessarily encourages them to ignore the political exterior. Therapy conflicts with fundamental feminist morality because it trades in social justice for a promise of feeling good, offers artificial human ties to people in desperate need of real love and caring, and has only empty answers to the problems of living. Therapy has made lesbians think that changing themselves is more important than changing the world. Or so Kitzinger and Perkins claim.

Most lesbian consumers and clinicians have not been convinced to abandon psychotherapy for good. But they have taken a hard look at what actually goes on in their therapeutic relationships. Do lesbian therapists have too much power over their clients? Do they impose white, middle-class values and manners (such as nonconfrontational "processing" of feelings) in the name of emotional well-being? Does therapy make poor and working-class women uncomfortable (if they can afford it in the first place) and deny the cultural heritages of women of color? Should therapy be a place to seek emergency aid, or should it be a permanent way of life? Discussion of these issues is lively and contentious. "Everywhere I looked," wrote Caryatis Cardea in a forum on lesbian therapy, "lesbians were going to therapists, becoming therapists, changing therapists, discussing their therapists, being abused by their therapists. If any other topic of conversation was introduced, it was phrased in the language of therapy."

In recent years, talk shows and legal scandals have made the public aware of abuses of various kinds, and lesbian therapeutic communities have been deeply involved in the exploration of childhood trauma and sexual abuse. Widely publicized cases of therapist-client sex have also raised real doubts about the trustworthiness of helping professionals

"Gay Bob" was billed as the world's first gay doll by its inventor, Harvey Rosenberg, upon its release in 1978. Though Rosenberg claims to have been very successful with the product, many parents remain uncomfortable with the notion of providing gay-positive influences for very young children.

both inside and outside of lesbian communities. A controversial recent book has renewed this debate by claiming that lesbians can be seriously harmed by well-intentioned therapists and raising questions about what the ethics of lesbian therapists and healers should be. In *When Boundaries Betray Us,* Carter Heyward, a lesbian Episcopal priest and widely published author on theological topics, narrates the story of her 18-month-long therapy with lesbian psychiatrist Elizabeth Farro (a pseudonym) in the late 1980s. Heyward and Farro hit it off right away. But the relationship turned sour when Farro, citing professional ethics, refused to comply with Heyward's repeated requests that the two women become friends outside of therapy. Heyward calls this stance "emotional betrayal and relational contempt." She felt spiritually "shattered, assaulted as truly as if I had been raped and beaten as a child and had split into pieces in order to survive." She describes how her "wounding" in therapy precipitated long years of painful self-reflection and recovery. Heyward even felt that she was going mad. "I had been *abused*—not sexually, but emotionally. It was becoming increasingly clear to me that abuse—damage, harm, violence—can result from a professional's refusal to be authentically present with those who seek help; and that such abuse can be triggered as surely by the drawing of boundaries too tightly as by a failure to draw them at all." That Farro would not be her friend meant that Farro was afraid of intimacy herself and—even worse—guilty of failing a patient in need.

It is tempting to dismiss Heyward as a self-involved, demanding woman who threw a very public temper tantrum because she did not get her way. (She was famous enough to be invited to tell her tale of therapeutic woe at the meetings of the American Psychiatric Association in 1991.) But the point Heyward is making—beyond her own personal story of therapy-gone-wrong—is that traditional ethical codes in psychotherapy that restrict mutual, social interaction between healers and their clients in the name of professionalism may actually perpetuate oppressive hierarchies, promote isolating individualism, and force separation between passionate women who long for meaningful interpersonal connection. The hard and fast rule prohibiting therapists and their clients from becoming friends (or lovers) is, Heyward writes, "a rule shaped professionally out of white men's fear of losing control." Lesbian therapists and therapy consumers should not passively accept that "boundaries" will protect them from abuse but actively work to free themselves from these "vestiges of psychospiritual bondage to patriarchal logic."

The number of psychotherapists still subscribing to the sickness model and the sticky ethics of gay-positive therapy are not the only issues worrying the post-Stonewall generation. The first cases of AIDS (reported by the Centers for Disease Control in 1981) re-invigorated vocal critics of the gay community—secular liberals and centrists as well as right-wing Christians—just when it seemed that psychiatry's change of mind about homosexuality's status as a mental illness should have finally started to lower the temperature of public homophobia. With the vast majority of early cases reported in gay and bisexual men (along with intravenous drug users and Haitians), the response of the mainstream press was either to ignore the disease entirely, presumably because of the marginal social status of the affected groups, or to shake an angry and judgmental finger at gay men themselves. "The poor homosexuals," wrote syndicated archconserva-tive columnist and 1992 presidential candidate Patrick Buchanan. "They have declared war on Nature, and now Nature is exacting an awful retribution."

Warnings about the disastrous consequences of promiscuity and the dangers to "innocent" (i.e., heterosexual) people of treating homosexu-ality as normal (or even tolerating it at all) threatened to reverse the ground that had been so hard won during the 1970s. Public opinion polls during the mid-1980s showed that a significant number of Ameri-cans (37 percent in one 1985 Gallup poll) had changed their minds for the worse about homosexuality because of AIDS. Although the emer-gence of militant AIDS activism and the vigorous lobbying of politi-cians, medical researchers, and the public at large have resulted in impressive gains since 1985, the epidemic has made it clear that doubts about the moral and cultural status of homosexuality remain both profound and widespread in American society, in spite of the psychiatric profession's official reversal. During the early years of the epidemic in particular, some gay men responded to calls to limit numbers of sexual partners and engage in "safe sex" as if they were nothing more than a retreat to the bad old days of the closet, when homosexuality was considered sick and experts dominated the national debate about the status of homosexuality. Other gay activists, however, demanded that urgent steps be taken—the closing of gay bathhouses, for example—to address the health crisis.

New research on the causes of homosexuality—this time biological rather than psychological—has also stirred controversy and disagreement among gay men and lesbians in recent years. During the 1970s and 1980s, biological approaches to mental illness and health gained much of the ground that psychoanalysis was losing. Advances in neurobiology, a field that studies the physiological structure and biochemistry of the brain, reenergized the old nature-versus-nurture debate, and this time the nature forces were much more likely to come out on top. The popularity of biological psychiatry was a general trend, and it influenced expert opinion on many subjects. Was manic-depression (now called bipolar disorder) triggered by chemical changes in the brain? Could certain "psychological" traits like inhibition be inborn and therefore not psychological at all? How and why could drugs like Prozac manage moods and even alter human personality?

Sexual orientation was also reassessed in light of biology's new vogue. One result was serious consideration of the possibility that homosexuals were born and not made—or at least born as well as made. Of course, many lesbians and gay men all along had been saying that they were "born that way" and had no choice in the matter, but this time it was the scientists who suggested that being gay might have more to do with biology than psychology. Experts searching for causes and cures should examine the body before meddling with the mind.

Sex change operations (now called sex reassignment surgery), which suggested that gender identity, at least, was entirely about the body, were old news. In 1952, Christine Jorgensen (a male-to-female transsexual) became world famous when she sold her story to the Hearst newspapers, launched a theatrical career, and wrote an autobiography. In recent years, transsexualism has continued to fascinate the American public, but surgery has not been the main focus of sexual science. Rather, scientists have investigated the hormonal, neural, and genetic components of sexual orientation.

John Money, a psychologist, has been a pioneer in the effort to understand how hormones affect gender identity, gender-specific behavior, and sexual preference. Since the early 1960s, he has studied hermaphrodites and other "experiments of nature" in whom biological sex (determined by chromosomes, hormones, and genitalia) and social sex (whether the person was reared as a boy or a girl) were not the same. In virtually all cases, it was the social sex that corresponded to the individual's own identity, and it was easier to alter the body (through surgery, for example) than it was to change a person's sense of themselves from male to female, or vice versa. (This forceful conviction that we are either male or female is sometimes referred to today as "core gender identity.") The conclusion Money reached was that gender and sexuality are the products of a complex dance between nature and culture at key turning points early in the process of human development. Whether certain hormonal switches are on or off can shape "the biology of learning" so that behaviors and identities become "imprinted and immutable." Money claims that if girls are exposed prenatally to unusually high levels of androgens (male hormones), for example, they will be less interested in typically "girl" activities later in life.

On the basis of animal studies, Money has also hypothesized that the "hormonalization" of the brain before birth is a significant factor in determining sexual orientation, though it does not determine the final outcome all by itself. All sorts of things in the lives of pregnant women—stress, food, drugs—may result in the brains of fetuses being masculinized or feminized and thus may set the stage for a homosexual or bisexual orientation later on. Just as people may be programmed prenatally to learn a language—even though they are not born speaking it—so too may people be primed for a particular sexual orientation before they are born. They may not be gay (certainly not in the adult sense) at birth, but they cannot alter their sexual orientation any more easily than they can switch their native language from English to Chinese.

Of course, hormones do not work all by themselves. They are controlled by the pituitary gland, which is controlled by the hypothalamus, a part of the brain. Scientists have therefore turned to the study of the brain itself. What impact do hormones have on its early development and on subsequent sexual orientation? Simon LeVay, a neuro-

Scientist Simon LeVay has been in the forefront of research into the question of whether homosexuality has a biological cause. LeVay has conducted research that indicates that a portion of the brain that possibly affects the sex drive may be significantly larger in male heterosexuals than in gay men.

biologist, has suggested that the brains of heterosexual and homosexual men may be different—literally. A gay man who accepted the Freudian analysis of homosexuality when he first encountered it as a teenager, LeVay has come to believe that homosexuality is mostly due to nature, with nurture playing only a very small role. He refers to statistical evidence that homosexuality runs in families. Studies have shown that identical twins (whose genes are exactly the same) are more likely to both end up gay than fraternal twins (whose genes are as different as any other set of siblings). LeVay speculates that precise markers for homosexuality may be found in the near future. In other words, the causes may be in our genes after all.

In an extremely controversial study published in *Science* in 1991, LeVay reported that a particular area of the hypothalamus was much larger, on average, in heterosexual than in homosexual men. To him, this finding suggested that the neurological mechanisms controlling sexual behavior in gay and straight men might be different, and that this difference was probably due to the influence of prenatal hormones. "Gay men simply don't have the brain cells to be attracted to women," he put it bluntly. Colleagues have criticized LeVay's study for relying exclusively on the brains of gay men who had died of AIDS (possibly it was the disease, rather than their homosexuality, that affected the hypothalamus), for overlooking lesbians and bisexuals entirely, and for numerous other weaknesses in his research method and conclusions.

Ironically, the new science of sexual orientation and the psychoanalytic consensus it has tried so hard to replace have a number of things in common. They both seek explanations in early development, either before birth or during the first few years of life—as if nothing that happens after age two or three can possibly make any difference. And both have clear social implications, though they wrap themselves in the language of the laboratory and swear allegiance only to science. Where the analytic perspective fueled a crusade to convert homosexuals to heterosexuality by curing the damage done to them in childhood, recent neurobiological studies point in the opposite direction: homosexuality *cannot* be changed, because it is a matter of genes and brain chemistry. Just as homophile advocates in the 1950s hoped that psychological enlightenment would bring toleration, many of today's gay rights advocates are willing to bet that biological discoveries will help their cause. (Of course, the possibility exists that this brave new science will inspire ominous new types of homophobia as well—for example, that genetic counseling will include information about preventing the conception of "gay children" or that "gay fetuses" will be aborted outright.) The optimistic theory is that if homosexuality can be shown

138

to be in humankind's genetic makeup, wired by hormones into the very structure of the brain, then it will finally prove that gay men and lesbians cannot help it, that they are not simply "choosing" to engage in unorthodox sex, purposely living perverse lives, and thumbing their noses at conventional sexual rules. Scientific evidence, it is still hoped, will convince heterosexuals that they have been wrong about gay Americans. At last they will agree that gay Americans deserve respect, legal equality, and social acceptance. After all, if homosexuality is "natural," is it not "normal" as well?

14

Normality and
Its Discontents

*"If God made you
gay, live that way with
dignity" reads the placard
raised by these activists
at a rally in front of
St. Patrick's Cathedral
in New York City.*

IN MODERN AMERICAN HISTORY, the destiny of
psychological experts and the fate of gay men and
lesbians have been closely connected. Psychological
experts have been important to gay people because
they decided who was mentally healthy and who was
not, and because their opinions mattered. Gay men and
lesbians have been important to psychological experts
because research about their lives has helped to extend
their authority over more people, and more behaviors,
than was ever the case in the past. Gay men and lesbians
have worked alongside experts like Alfred Kinsey and
Evelyn Hooker, whose work was compatible with
reform, and have engineered showdowns with experts
like Irving Bieber and Charles Socarides, whose work
distorted the gay experience and turned it into an
illness. There have been dramatic twists and turns
in this strange relationship, but one thing has not

changed. During World War II and the McCarthy era, in the fight over the *DSM* and the campaign to force a gay-affirmative psychology, psychological experts and members of the gay community have always staked out the very same territory: normality.

Normality has been a central goal for the gay movement because being normal has promised change, whereas being abnormal seemed to offer a future just like the homophobic past. Normality can backfire, however, as some gay men and lesbians have pointed out. It is easily confused with being respectable or being the same as everyone else, which in the American imagination implies behaving politely, dressing appropriately, and belonging to the middle class. If it means going out of our way to raise no eyebrows at all, being normal can make it extremely difficult to acknowledge that gay people *are* different—different from heterosexuals and also different from other gay men and lesbians.

Today's controversies about how visible drag queens and dykes on bikes should be in Gay Pride marches and whether or not to support the in-your-face tactics of groups like ACT-UP and Queer Nation are not new, though they are far more likely to be mentioned on the network news than in the past, when they appeared only in the pages of gay community newspapers. Gay people have always been divided on the question of what image to present to America, and that division has had everything to do with appearing normal. "We have spent 20 years convincing people that homosexuals are no different than anyone else," Los Angeles activist Don Slater announced with exasperation, "and here these kids come along and reinforce what society thought all along—that homosexuals are different, that they're 'queer.' 'Gay' is good! To hell with that."

Slater expressed his views in 1970. Today, little has changed, except that the growing visibility and size of the gay movement have made it easier for gay men and lesbians—especially if they came of age in the post-Stonewall years—to flaunt their uniqueness and shout at the top of their lungs: "We're here, we're queer, we're fabulous, get used to it!" Still, there are many who desire nothing more than to blend in and live ordinary lives without interference from church or state. In a society

Wally McMillan (left) and Richard Faust embrace on the steps of city hall in San Francisco on February 14, 1991, after registering as domestic partners under a new city ordinance. In some areas of the country, legislation now makes it possible for gay and lesbian couples to legally formalize their commitment to one another.

where gay people have lost jobs and families and have been accused of subverting the family and promoting communism, the lure of normality is easy to understand.

But not all gay men and lesbians aspire to long-term, monogamous "marriages," home ownership, and 2.5 children. Some gay men and lesbians will never be able to have these things because they lack opportunities or resources. Others simply do not want them. There are gay men and lesbians for whom this type of normality is boring and who would rather push the limits of what is acceptable in sexual behavior, dress, and cultural expression. There is something wrong with a vision of normality that leaves these people on the margin as the new deviants of the 1990s. Yet it is partly because of the history recounted in this book—because of strenuous efforts over many decades to be accepted as normal—that some gay men and lesbians can have many lovers if they so desire, engage in kinky sex, and wear feathers and leather—all without feeling like "perverts" and being denounced as emotionally "sick." Because gay men and lesbians have come to think of homosexuality as a healthy variant of normal human sexuality, it is much easier than it used to be to reject and ridicule normality as a collective goal. When almost everybody thought homosexuals were ill, and many gays and lesbians felt that way themselves, being seen and accepted as normal was essential, urgent, and meaningful for most gay and lesbian Americans. Now that gay and lesbian Americans are approaching normal, normality has lost some of its shine. It can even be taken for granted.

If the history recounted in this book has shown anything, it has demonstrated that the normality of homosexuality must not be taken for granted. The fact that gay men and lesbians are as psychologically healthy (and unhealthy) as other human beings is not something that scientists have finally discovered after decades of unfortunate errors, nor is it something that people automatically understand. Normality and abnormality are products of culture, and we all learn—as children and adults—to evaluate ourselves and one another through their lenses. Because American culture has changed a great deal over the past 50 years, this society's view of who is normal or abnormal has also changed. At every moment, though, this view has made a huge difference in how gay and lesbian Americans feel about themselves. Whether we feel mentally balanced or emotionally disturbed, whether we accept our sexual feelings or despise them—these have not been matters of luck or fate, any more than they have been technical questions best left to experts. People have struggled for and against consensus views of normality on the battleground of social history and social conflict.

The current state of gay-friendly psychology is something to be proud of, and it certainly has been hard won. But the history of psychology and homosexuality shows that it is probably too soon to conclude that the war has been won. Relying too heavily on the kindness of professional strangers has been an error in the past, and it is still an error today. Whether the future will hold psychological well-being or misery for gay and lesbian Americans has not been permanently decided. "Normality" is in our own hands.

◼ *Further Reading* ◼

Bayer, Ronald. *Homosexuality and American Psychiatry: The Politics of Diagnosis*. Princeton, NJ: Princeton University Press, 1987.

Bergler, Edmund. *Homosexuality: Disease or Way of Life?* New York: Collier, 1956.

Bérubé, Allan. *Coming Out Under Fire: The History of Gay Men and Women in World War II*. New York: Free Press, 1990.

Bieber, Irving. *Homosexuality: A Psychoanalytic Study*. Northvale, NJ: Jason Aronson, 1988.

Duberman, Martin. *Cures: A Gay Man's Odyssey*. New York: Dutton, 1991.

Garnets, Linda D., and Douglas C. Kimmel. *Psychological Perspectives on Lesbian & Gay Male Experiences*. New York: Columbia University Press, 1993.

Irvine, Janice. *Disorders of Desire: Sex and Gender in Modern American Sexology*. Philadelphia: Temple University Press, 1990.

LeVay, Simon. *The Sexual Brain*. Cambridge, MA: MIT Press, 1993.

Marcus, Eric. *Making History: The Struggle for Gay and Lesbian Equal Rights, 1945–1990, An Oral History*. New York: Harper Perennial, 1992.

Nicolosi, Joseph. *Reparative Therapy of Male Homosexuality: A New Clinical Approach*. Northvale, NJ: Jason Aronson, 1991.

▣ *Index* ▣

Ellen Herman lives in Boston with her family, where she teaches at Harvard University in the social studies program. A frequent contributor to the gay and lesbian press on a range of topics, she was also a member of the organizing committee for OutWrite 1992, the national conference for gay and lesbian writers. Her book *The Romance of American Psychology: Political Culture in the Age of Experts* is published by the University of California Press. She is currently working on a book about psychotherapy, tentatively titled *The Growth Industry.*

Martin Duberman is Distinguished Professor of History at the Graduate Center for the City University of New York and the founder and director of the Center for Gay and Lesbian Studies. One of the country's foremost historians, he is the author of 15 books and numerous articles and essays. He has won the Bancroft Prize for *Charles Francis Adams* (1960); two Lambda awards for *Hidden from History: Reclaiming the Gay and Lesbian Past,* an anthology that he coedited; and a special award from the National Academy of Arts and Letters for his overall "contributions to literature." His play *In White America* won the Vernon Rice/Drama Desk Award in 1964. His other works include *James Russell Lowell* (1966), *Black Mountain: An Exploration in Community* (1972), *Paul Robeson* (1989), *Cures: A Gay Man's Odyssey* (1991), and *Stonewall* (1993).

Professor Duberman received his Ph.D. in history from Harvard University in 1957 and served as professor of history at Yale University and Princeton University from 1957 until 1972, when he assumed his present position at the City University of New York.